Pope John Paul II

reaching out across borders

ISBN 0-13-140803-8

Pope John Paul II

reaching out across borders

REUTERS

Published by **Prentice Hall**

Library of Congress Cataloging-in-Publication Data

A CIP catalog record for this book can be obtained from the Library of Congress

Publisher: Tim Moore
Executive editor: Jim Boyd
Director of production: Sophie Papanikolaou
Production supervisor: Patti Guerrieri
Marketing manager: John Pierce
Manufacturing manager: Alexis Heydt-Long

Editorial assistant: Linda Ramagnano
Cover design director: Jerry Votta
Cover designer: Anthony Gemmellaro
Art director: Gail Cocker-Bogusz
Interior design: Meg Van Arsdale
Page layout: Gail Cocker-Bogusz and Meg Van Arsdale

Reuters
Executive editor: Stephen Jukes
Coordinating editor: Peter Millership
Associate editor: Philip Pullella
Commercial manager: Alisa Bowen
Front cover art photographer: Gary Hershorn
Cover photo copyright © 2002 Reuters

In compiling this book, thanks go to many people. At Reuters, David Cutler, Giles Elgood, Mikhail Evstafiev, Nelson Graves, Gary Hershorn, Paul Holmes, Sean Maguire, David Storey, Mike Tyler, Christopher Wilson; thanks also go to Iona Millership.

© 2003 Reuters
Published by Pearson Education Inc.
Publishing as Reuters Prentice Hall
Upper Saddle River, NJ 07458

Prentice Hall books are widely used by corporations and government agencies
for training, marketing and resale.

For information regarding corporate and government bulk discounts please contact:
Corporate and Government Sales (800) 382-3419, or corpsales@pearsontechgroupl.com.

Printed in the United States of America

10 9 8 7 6 5 4 3 2 1

ISBN 0-13-140803-8

Pearson Education LTD.
Pearson Education Australia PTY, Limited
Pearson Education Singapore, Pte. Ltd.
Pearson Education North Asia Ltd.
Pearson Education Canada, Ltd.
Pearson Educación de Mexico, S.A. de C.V.
Pearson Education—Japan
Pearson Education Malaysia, Pte. Ltd.

Contents

A Great Humanist

by Mikhail Gorbachev

People say things are clearer when one can stand back and view events with the advantage of time.

It is true that historic perspective is vital to appreciate the stature of an individual and his vision. Nearly a quarter of a century of pastoral activity by His Holiness John Paul II allows us to give real credit to this remarkable man.

I first met Pope John Paul 14 years ago. That meeting was followed by more talks and an exchange of letters and ideas. The impressions I had of the pope after that first meeting at the Vatican on December 1, 1989, were reinforced over time.

Then, as now, I am convinced that John Paul's mission is to serve mankind. His motives are never mundane, his thoughts know no borders.

The pontiff's beliefs and actions are driven by a passionate desire to improve the spiritual, moral and material world of each person, to contribute to the goal of a better, more peaceful world and a just international order. That is what dominates the spiritual and political agenda of John Paul.

This helps us to understand his judgment of societies that used to be called socialist and of today's capitalist societies, steeped in liberal fundamentalism.

This inspires his ardent desire for peace and justice, his decisive condemnation of war and violence, including terrorism. This is the source of his firm defense of human life in harmony with nature.

Here is a great humanist who carries out his mission without hesitation: such a man is John Paul. One can only marvel at his perseverance, his energy and his vitality.

I wish from the bottom of my heart that Heaven allows him to serve mankind under God's guidance for as long as possible.

Mikhail Gorbachev

last president of the
Soviet Union and a
Nobel Peace Prize winner

To Renew the Face of the Earth

by Lech Walesa

Defeating communism and ending the Cold War was a success with many fathers. All of them deserve credit for helping to achieve this peacefully. But it is impossible not to bow, as a dutiful son, before the paramount champion of the cause of freedom—Pope John Paul. I do so looking back at the miracle the pope wrought, which gave meaning and confidence to our efforts and changed the face of the world.

During his first pilgrimage to Poland, the Holy Father uttered two sentences of great significance: "Be not afraid," and "Renew the face of the earth. This earth." The pope showed us how numerous we were and showed us the strength and power we had if we joined together as one. We stopped being afraid and gathered together 10 million people in our trade union, Solidarity, which changed the face of this earth. Communism's real strength until then had been the weakness of society and our isolation as individuals. Apart from its brute force—the militia, army and tanks—our social weakness and separateness were the main pillars of communist strength. In 1979 and 1980 these pillars collapsed in Poland. And in their place stood the great hope contained in the word *Solidarność* (Solidarity).

They tried to take it away from us. That was the aim of martial law. But they did not succeed. Martial law failed to destroy our unity. Many of us had our faith severely tested, but they could not take away our hope. There was a lot of pain at the loss of dear ones and much longing for those imprisoned. But above all they could not take away from us our solidarity. They cost us time and kept us from achieving freedom for a while. It finally came because we could not be broken, we survived. In the hardest moments we always had the words of the Holy Father in our minds. And still we wanted to change the face of this earth. After his pilgrimage to his native land, we were fortified and strengthened. We felt that the cause of freedom was our cause and the cause of millions of people desiring change.

The pope is with us now as he was then. Now it is a new world. He helps us face the problems of today with his whole personality and whole heart. In difficult times of destruction and violence, he calls for solidarity among mankind, for building a civilization of love, for sympathy with those in need, for religious and cultural dialogue and for an awakening of the consciences of men. He is rescuing morality in a globalizing world. It gives us hope of building a real and lasting peace. Because, above all, hope is what we need.

Lech Walesa

former president of Poland,
first leader of the Solidarity trade union movement and a
Nobel Peace Prize winner

The kiss. At his weekly general audience, November 28, 2001.
Paolo Cocco/Reuters

Pope John Paul II

reaching out across borders

From Wooden Clogs to the Shoes of the Fisherman

Philip Pullella

In August 2002, during a visit to his native Poland, Pope John Paul consecrated a new basilica on the outskirts of his beloved Krakow. He had written his address weeks before at the Vatican, but as he delivered it he paused. Looking out over the crowd, he was transported back almost a lifetime to the dark days of World War Two. In his mind's eye, a young man trudged through the biting cold of a southern Polish winter, his lips moving in solitary prayer as he made his way to work in a chemicals plant commandeered by Nazi occupiers outside Krakow. Thinking aloud, the pope recalled that the young man wore wooden clogs. Sixty-two years after walking that lonely road, Karol Wojtyla sat at the service on an ivory-colored, padded throne, the leader of one billion Roman Catholics. He had cemented his place in history as a spiritual slayer of communism, survived an assassin's bullets and become one of the most recognized faces on the planet. "Who would have thought that someone in those wooden shoes would one day be consecrating this basilica?" he asked, both in wonder and thanksgiving. Loudspeakers carried his trembling voice outside the church and into fields filled with pilgrims. Too far away to see even the door of the basilica, they were kneeling just the same. The man who once wore clogs was a son of the soil their knees were pressing against and the successor to St. Peter, the Apostle who cast his nets into the Sea of Galilee 2,000 years ago; he now wore the Shoes of the Fisherman.

In the world of business, Karol Wojtyla's story would be one of rags to riches, the tale of a poor boy who started out in the mailroom and defied the odds to reach the top. A pope is "chief executive officer" of the oldest continuously run institution in history, and it is arguably the loneliest position in the world. He is leader of a Church that has given history some of its greatest saints, artists and thinkers as well as some of its most notorious sinners, warmongers and rogues. He is "CEO" of an organization that runs everything from soaring urban basilicas to one-room village chapels, from universities to leper colonies, from hospitals with cutting-edge technology in Manhattan to tin-roofed clinics in the slums of Rio de Janeiro. The orders that emanate under the pope's auspices from the frescoed offices of the Church's central administration at the Vatican touch on all aspects of Catholic life. They range from matters of sexual morality to bioethics, from priests in politics to women in the church, from the proper use of something as intimate as the sacrament of confession to how best to reach millions via something as public as the Internet. A supreme sovereign in a 108-acre walled city–state he has sometimes called a "prison," the pope can command the world stage but can also cut a solitary figure at the window from where he looks out over St. Peter's Square. He can be compared to Christ looking out from his wooden cross on Golgotha—loved by some, despised by others, misunderstood by many, but watched by all. Christ entrusted his Church to Peter and gave him the Keys to the Kingdom. Nearly 2,000 years and 263 popes later, on October 16, 1978, Karol Wojtyla was elected the first non-Italian pope in more than 455 years and the youngest for 150 years. At 58, it became his turn to be the Keeper of the Keys.

Pastor, Statesman, Bishop

On the afternoon of September 10, 1987, a gleaming jumbo jet in the white, green and red livery of the Italian airline Alitalia landed at Miami International Airport ending a 10-hour flight from Rome. After thrusting the engines into reverse, the pilot and copilot reached out of the windows of the cockpit to decorate the nose of the Boeing 747 with the yellow and white Vatican flag. The pope is a religious leader, but he is also a head of state. Awaiting him on the tarmac was President Ronald Reagan. The pope and Reagan saw the world in different terms yet shared the same abhorrence of communism. At a private meeting in a Mediterranean-style mansion, they talked about U.S. relations with the Soviet Union and about its leader, Mikhail Gorbachev, who was making a name for himself with his *perestroika* and *glasnost* policies. The pope told Reagan of his dream of a Europe undivided, as he liked to put it, "from the Atlantic to the Urals." Three months earlier, Reagan visited Berlin, the divided city on the front line of the Cold War, and issued his famous challenge: "Mr. Gorbachev, tear down this wall." George Herbert Walker Bush was vice president at the time. When he succeeded Reagan in 1989, the Berlin Wall would come tumbling down. The lives of four men— Reagan, Bush, Gorbachev and Wojtyla—were converging in a way that would change history.

That same evening in Miami, John Paul met with representatives of priests' councils from across the United States. The atmosphere was light and friendly, but some of the messages from the priests were direct. One of them, Father Frank McNulty, spoke of the yearning of women in the Catholic Church to achieve

To the city and the world. St. Peter's Square on Easter Sunday for the traditional Urbi et Orbi address, April 7, 1996.
Vatican photo

positions of greater responsibility. Some saw McNulty's speech as a clear call to open the priesthood to women, which the Church says it cannot do. Noting McNulty's Irish name, John Paul responded with the title of a famous song about a town in Ireland. "It's a long way to Tipperary," he said. Delivered with the timing of the actor he once was, John Paul brought the house down with laughter. Both sides had made their point. But the pope had the final word.

The pope's first few hours on the ground during his visit to the United States provided a microcosm of his various roles. He read his arrival address as pastor to the 65 million Roman Catholics in the United States. In it he spoke of his concern as a father figure for the growing number of poor and Hispanics left behind during the "Me Generation" that coincided with Reagan's presidency. At his private talks with Reagan, he went one on one with the leader of the world's most powerful nation on matters of global political consequence. At his meeting with his priests, he assumed

Deep in prayer. Basilica of St. Remy, Reims, France,
September 22, 1996. Paul Hanna/Reuters

Pope John Paul II: timeline

1920 May 18 – Born Karol Jozef Wojtyla, in Wadowice, Poland

1939 Nazis invade Poland, World War Two begins

1946 Ordained in Krakow, completed studies at pontifical universities in Rome and returns to Poland

1958 Consecrated assistant Bishop of Krakow

1964 Named Archbishop of Krakow

1967 Made a cardinal by Pope Paul VI

1978 October 16 – Elected the first non-Italian pope since Adrian VI. Inaugurated six days later

1979 Returns to Poland. The trip becomes a major factor in the rise of the Solidarity movement

1981 May 13 – Turkish gunman Mehmet Ali Agca shoots and severely wounds the pope in St. Peter's Square. Emergency surgery at a Rome hospital saves his life

1982 On eve of the first anniversary of Agca's assassination attempt, a rebel Spanish priest tries to stab the pope at the Marian shrine in Fatima, Portugal. The pope is not harmed

1982 Visits Britain. In a major move towards reconciliation with Anglicans he prays with the Archbishop of Canterbury

1986 Makes first visit by a pontiff to a synagogue. Prays with Rome's chief rabbi in a major advance in Catholic-Jewish relations

1989 The pope and the Archbishop of Canterbury pledge to work to resume unity between Anglican and Roman Catholic Churches

1989 Historic meeting with Soviet President Mikhail Gorbachev turns 70 years of atheist ideology on its head

1991 Makes first trip to his homeland since collapse of communism

1992 Undergoes major surgery to remove large intestinal tumor

1992 The Anglican Church's decision to allow women priests brings relations with the Vatican to a new low

1992 Issues Roman Catholic Church's new Universal Catechism – the first in nearly five centuries

1993 The Vatican and Israel forge full diplomatic ties in the most important move towards ending nearly 2,000 years of distrust between Christians and Jews

1994 Undergoes bone replacement surgery after breaking his leg in a fall at the Vatican

1994 In a letter to the world's Catholic bishops, the pope forcefully reaffirms Catholic Church's ban on women priests

1995 Papal document Evangelium Vitae (the Gospel of Life) calls for non-violent opposition by all Christians to abortion and euthanasia

1998 The Vatican apologizes to Jews for Catholics who failed to do enough to stop Nazi persecution

2000 The pope asks forgiveness for the past sins of his Church, including its treatment of Jews, heretics, women and minorities

2000 Makes historic trip to the Holy Land, visiting holy sites in Israel and the Palestinian territories

2000 During papal visit to Fatima, Portugal, the Vatican reveals the so-called "Third Secret of Fatima" predicting the attempt on the pope's life in 1981

2001 In first message to world via the Internet, the pope apologizes to victims of sex abuse by priests and other clergy

2002 In his annual "state of the world" address, the pope says the fight against terrorism is legitimate and that killing in God's name is blasphemy

2002 Summons U.S. Roman Catholic Cardinals in emergency summit to deal with child sex scandal rocking the American Church

2002 October 16 – Marks his 24th anniversary of being elected pope

Popes since Adrian VI

Adrian VI	1522–23
Clement VII	1523–34
Paul III	1534–49
Julius III	1550–55
Marcellus II	1555
Paul IV	1555–59
Pius IV	1559–65
St. Pius V	1566–72
Gregory XIII	1572–85
Sixtus V	1585–90
Urban VII	1590
Gregory XIV	1590–91
Innocent IX	1591
Clement VIII	1592–1605
Leo XI	1605
Paul V	1605–21
Gregory XV	1621–23
Urban VIII	1623–44
Innocent X	1644–55
Alexander VII	1655–67
Clement IX	1667–69
Clement X	1670–76
Blessed Innocent XI	1676–89
Alexander VIII	1689–91
Innocent XII	1691–1700
Clement XI	1700–21
Innocent XIII	1721–24
Benedict XIII	1724–30
Clement XII	1730–40
Benedict XIV	1740–58
Clement XIII	1758–69
Clement XIV	1769–74
Pius VI	1775–99
Pius VII	1800–23
Leo XII	1823–29
Pius VIII	1829–30
Gregory XVI	1831–46
Blessed Pius IX	1846–78
Leo XIII	1878–1903
St. Pius X	1903–14
Benedict XV	1914–22
Pius XI	1922–39
Pius XII	1939–58
Blessed John XXIII	1958–63
Paul VI	1963–78
John Paul I	1978
John Paul II	**1978–**

Source: Reuters

the role of company executive, listening to the concerns of the staff and delivering the papal equivalent of a corporate pep talk.

A Church Divided

John Paul saw himself as bishop to the world. His pastoral style did not change much after his election. Before 1978, when his diocese was Krakow, he made it a point to visit parishes regularly. After his election as pontiff, every bit of land where a Catholic might dwell became a corner of his super-diocese. But whether he was flying to the other side of the world or traveling within Italy, the pope tended to a Church divided. Perhaps it was no more divided than in periods of its tortuous past, but the modern media made it possible for Catholics around the world to take sides in debates that were long the preserve of an elite. In 1985, for example, Leonardo Boff, a Franciscan priest who had provoked the Vatican's ire over some of his writings on "liberation theology," was summoned to Rome from Brazil and questioned by the Congregation for the Doctrine of the Faith, the successor to the department once known as the Inquisition. The Vatican criticized Boff and other "liberation theologians" for using Marxist analysis in their writings and thus, the argument went, supporting a divisive and potentially violent class struggle. Boff found a crowd of reporters swarming around him when he emerged from the Vatican after the meeting. In a scene worthy of a Fellini film, journalists and photographers on motor scooters chased his car to a convent in Rome's Aurelio quarter up the hill from the Vatican. Less than an hour after the meeting was over, his voice was broadcast on Brazilian radio, and that night Boff, with his shock of wavy hair, brown Franciscan habit and academic-looking tortoise shell glasses, defended his views on television around the world. By contrast, when Galileo was dragged before the Inquisition in 1633 for defending the Copernican theory that the earth revolved around the sun, most Catholics did not learn of the trial for decades. Just as the Vietnam War became the first war to be delivered into living rooms through television, John Paul's was the first papacy to be delivered into living rooms. The media was midwife to the most visible papacy in history and perhaps the most significant, eventful and consequential since the Reformation.

Nuns thrilled to be close to the pope during his mountain holiday in Italy's Val d'Aosta region, July 16, 2000. Claudio Papi/Reuters

In his role as pastor, the pope found that nearly everyone loved the messenger but not everyone loved the message. In advanced countries such as the United States and throughout Western Europe, many in the adoring crowds wept with joy when they saw the pope, whom they truly considered Christ's vicar on earth. But they also dissented, in private or in public, from some of the Church's teachings. Many used artificial birth control instead of the natural family planning methods approved by the Church, or disagreed with its ban on women priests and its branding of homosexual activity as a "disorder." Still, they considered themselves not only Catholics but in some cases, good Catholics. We in the media, with our insatiable appetite for buzzwords, called this "cafeteria Catholicism"—take what you want and leave the rest. The pope opposed this view, but it did not surprise him. He once said: "I am not the first against whom there was disagreement. Who was the first? Jesus Christ." That statement spoke volumes about an institution that thinks in centuries and has survived down the ages without having to reinvent itself at each historical turn, each social upheaval.

In the months before John Paul's 1987 trip to the United States, American Catholics were caught up in the so-called Curran affair. Father Charles Curran, who taught at the Catholic University of America in Washington, DC, had openly questioned the Church's teachings on a range of sexual issues. Curran called his observations "faithful dissent," asserting that it was legitimate to question such teachings because they had not been infallibly defined. After Curran refused to recant, Cardinal Joseph Ratzinger, the head of the Congregation for the Doctrine of the Faith, ruled that he could no longer teach as a theologian in a Catholic institution. While conservative Catholics applauded, the affair became a cause celebre for many other Catholics who said their Church should change more with the times. The Vatican's message was that the rules could not be bent simply because they were difficult to observe. "The Catholic Church is not a democratic institution," the pope said at the time. "It is an institution governed by Jesus Christ. We are only servants of one chief, of one pastor. We are only his instruments, his envoys."

The Cry of the Poor

Most Catholics in the developing world had never heard of Curran, Ratzinger or any of the names that were dropped on Washington's Georgetown academic cocktail party circuit that year. Yet they too were Catholics. One of these was a woman who lived in a notorious slum known as El Guasmo, near Guayaquil, Ecuador, which the pope visited in 1985. The bamboo houses were built on stilts. In the rainy season, water mixed with raw sewage. The only decoration in the woman's one-room house was a picture of the pope taken from a magazine. In El Guasmo and elsewhere in Latin America, Africa and Asia, the recurring themes on all of the pope's trips were human rights and the abolition of poverty. He supported agrarian reform in Brazil and Indian rights in Mexico, backed the struggle of unemployed miners in Bolivia and raised his fist in anger at the Maoist Shining Path guerrillas who were terrorizing the peasants of the Peruvian highlands. But as priests who took up leftist causes in Latin America were to learn, they

would have to help the poor his way. The gospel of Jesus Christ, the pope would often say in those turbulent years, was the only ideology they needed. It was enough to help get him through Nazism and communism in Poland and it should be enough for them. "I have understood what exploitation is, and I have immediately put myself on the side of the poor, the disinherited, the oppressed, the alienated and the defenseless," he told Polish–Italian journalist Jas Gawronski. "The powerful in this world do not always look favorably on a pope like that."

Some critics said the pope was wrong even to meet with some of the "powerful in this world," men such as Philippines President Ferdinand Marcos, Haitian dictator Jean-Claude "Baby Doc" Duvalier, Chilean President General Augusto Pinochet and South Africa's leaders before the end of apartheid. But the pope always felt that dialogue was supremely better than public revulsion or isolation. He is known to have read some strong-arm leaders the riot act in their private meetings after smiling for the cameras in public. "I know for a fact that the pope has been very clear and forceful in closed-door meetings with some world leaders," said Monsignor Renato Boccardo, a senior Vatican official who is the chief organizer of papal trips. Asked once if by meeting with a dictator he was not granting recognition or risking being exploited, the pope responded: "When was a visit by the pope not exploited?" Although an intellectual, a poet, an actor, a dramatist and a prolific writer, John Paul's affinity with Catholics in the developing world was at least in part based on his love for the "popular piety" that was prevalent in the Poland of his youth—the processions through the streets while singing and carrying statues of the Madonna, praying the rosary in public, walking through the forests while contemplating the 14 Stations of the Cross that recall events in Christ's passion and death. To the pope, these were not oversimplifications constructed to placate peasants or mesmerize the masses but seeds of faith. In the late 20th century they were disappearing from many places around the world, but they were still played out in Latin America. And they often played out in the mind of Karol Wojtyla when he remembered his youth in Poland.

A Polish Boy

You can take the boy out of Poland, but you can't take Poland out of the boy. It is impossible to overstate the significance Poland had on the life of the pope and equally impossible to overstate the significance he has had on modern Poland. His enormous stature has few parallels in the country's rich and troubled history of partition, resistance and occupation. Another famous son, Nicolaus Copernicus, revolutionized astronomy, but the pope revolutionized the self-esteem of Poles. Romantic 19th century composers such as Fryderyk Chopin and poets like Adam Mickiewicz may have interpreted the rebellious Polish spirit, but many Poles believe the pope liberated it. The pope believes that providence has a divine hand in everything. The important thing was being able to recognize it and act on it. So it was that in 1980 a Polish electrician named Lech Walesa, from the Gdansk shipyards, found the courage to do the unthinkable—declare a strike in a communist country. The pope supported him from Rome. Despite the many trials and tribulations of his homeland—including two years of martial law—he provided the fuel to keep the fire of freedom alive. Using his world pulpit to defend his homeland, he injected his countrymen with the courage that toppled communism in 1989. As Poland went, so went Eastern Europe. The domino effect that would sweep across the region was a mostly nonviolent social revolution. On December 1, 1989, Gorbachev met the pope at the Vatican and praised him as a moral leader. It was an event that turned more than 70 years of Soviet ideology on its head. There is no way of knowing how history would have played out if the pope had kept silent or if he had been more cautious in his comments. Perhaps Poland, 1980, would have gone down as just another blip on the radar of the history of communism, like the Hungarian Uprising in 1956 or the Prague Spring in 1968. The pope was convinced that the 1980 shipyards strike was the start of something big. But he was equally convinced that first he and his Church would have to suffer some more.

Suffering for the Kingdom

Suffering. It is a byword of Karol Wojtyla's life and papacy. The extraordinary catalog of pain—both emotional and physical—began when he was only eight years old. By the time he was a young man, he already was convinced there was great spiritual significance and redemptive meaning to suffering. The circumstances of his early life would be enough to make many people doubt God's very existence,

Age and youth. The pope and a child who received communion from him at a mass in St. Peter's Basilica, May 24, 2001. Paolo Cocco/Reuters

In the footsteps of Jesus. At Korazim, Israel, where Jesus gave his Sermon on the Mount. March 24, 2000.
Vincenzo Pinto/Reuters

but for the young Lolek, as his friends called him, it was part of the proof. A month before his ninth birthday, Karol Wojtyla lost his mother. Of frail health from birth, Emilia Kaczorowska succumbed to an inflammation of the heart on April 13, 1929, just before her 45th birthday. In 1932 his elder brother Edmund, a doctor who was the family's pride and Karol Wojtyla's personal hero, died of scarlet fever. Karol Wojtyla was only 12. His father, the elder Karol, a retired noncommissioned officer in the Austro–Hungarian army, became the center of his universe. First in their hometown of Wadowice and later in Krakow—where they moved in 1938 so Karol could be close to the Jagiellonian University—prayer and austerity were watchwords in the private lives of the two men. "Day after day I was able to observe the austere way in which he lived," the pope wrote in his 1996 memoir *Gift and Mystery*. "By profession he was a soldier and, after my mother's death, his life became one of constant prayer. Sometimes I would wake up during the night and find my father on his knees, just as I would always see him kneeling in the parish church." A year after the two moved to Krakow, Germany invaded Poland from the west and the Soviet Union advanced from the east. On October 5, 1939, little more than a month after the war began, Hitler reviewed his troops in Warsaw and the possibility of a Polish genocide was in the air. To avoid deportation, Karol worked as a manual laborer for the Solvay chemical company, first in the Zakrzowek quarry and later in the Borek Falecki plant. The experience of sweat on the brow and shoveling limestone would allow him to be called the first "worker pope" in modern history. It set him apart from those who had never known the rigors of manual labor, distinct from those groomed from birth for great things in good Italian families. "I was present when, during the detonation of a dynamite charge, some rocks struck a worker and killed him," he wrote in his memoir. "The experience left a profound impression on me." On February 18, 1941, Karol Wojtyla returned home to the damp basement apartment he shared with his father to find that the center of his universe was gone. Karol Wojtyla senior had been in bed for two months and died while his son was working. The pope would later tell the French writer André Frossard: "At 20, I had already lost all the people I loved, and even those I might have loved, like my older sister, who died six years before I was born." For the next four years until the end of the war, Wojtyla saw death all around him in Krakow. "Sometimes I would ask myself: so many young people of my own age are losing their lives, why not me? Today I know that it was not mere chance," he wrote in *Gift and Mystery*.

After the war, nearly half a century of communist oppression began. Yet even after Cardinal Karol Wojtyla left his beloved Poland, the suffering was not to end. On October 12, 1978, a day before Wojtyla entered the conclave of cardinals from which he would emerge as pope, his old friend, Bishop Andrzej Maria Deskur, suffered a massive stroke in Rome. Later, Wojtyla was to see this too as a personal suffering linked somehow by divine providence to his election, as added weight on the cross he felt he had to bear. Suffering, the pope believed, could become a source of inner peace and even spiritual joy. And for the pope there would be much more.

Blood in St. Peter's Square

At 5:17 p.m. on May 13, 1981, the pope was standing in his white "popemobile," riding through St. Peter's Square to the steps of Christendom's largest church to begin his weekly general audience. The popemobile slowed so he could kiss Sara Bartoli, a little girl who was holding a balloon. Mehmet Ali Agca, a 23-year-old Turk, drew a Browning 9mm pistol and fired two shots from about three yards. One bullet hit the pope in the abdomen; the other struck his right elbow and his left index finger. The bullets continued their trajectories to hit two American tourists, Anne Odre and Rose Hall. The pope lost consciousness when he reached the Gemelli Hospital, and his longtime secretary, Monsignor Stanislaw Dziwisz, administered the sacrament of the sick, once known as Extreme Unction, or The Last Rites. Five-and-a-half hours of surgery by Dr. Francesco Crucitti saved his life. More than 15,000 telegrams expressing shock arrived in the Vatican that day. One was from Soviet leader Leonid Brezhnev.

The pope publicly forgave Agca in a radio address from his hospital bed four days later, saying he was "praying for that brother who shot me." Agca was sentenced to life in prison on July 22. Few in the Vatican or at the White House believed Agca acted alone. But in 1985 a second trial failed to provide sufficient evidence to convict three Turks and three Bulgarians of having conspired with Agca to kill the pope. The Bulgarian Connection—the theory that the Soviet KGB had contracted the Bulgarian secret services to

(continued on page 14)

Mountains' majesty. Contemplating the Dolomites during a holiday in northern Italy, July 15, 1996.
Vatican photo

The Day the Pope Was Shot

By Philip Pullella

"The pope has been shot. Take me to St. Peter's Square. I'll pay you anything you want."

Those were the words I shouted to a teenager as I jumped on the back of his Vespa scooter in Rome's Largo Argentina, a square about halfway between my office and the Vatican. It was May 13, 1981. My editor had heard on a live Vatican Radio broadcast that shots had rung out in St. Peter's Square as Pope John Paul was starting his weekly audience. He heard the excited radio commentator say that the pope had fallen in his popemobile and that it was rushing back inside the Vatican walls.

I rushed out of our office near the Trevi Fountain and into a taxi. Impatient with the traffic, I left the taxi at Largo Argentina and stopped the teenager on his Vespa. I told him to run the red lights. As we crossed the Tiber River at the Vittorio Bridge, I noticed that police had set up a roadblock at the start of Via della Conciliazione, the broad boulevard that runs from the Tiber to the Vatican.

"Slow down but don't stop," I told the boy. "They won't shoot us." As we passed the police, I pulled out my Vatican press credentials and shouted to the policeman: "I'm with the Vatican." It worked and we sped through. All the time I was thinking, "What if?".

In St. Peter's Square, I found an atmosphere of stunned disbelief. Men, women and nuns were sobbing everywhere.

Children were in tears because their parents were crying and shaken, their heads in their hands. People felt forlorn. Sirens wailed. On a platform in front of the basilica, the pope's white throne languished empty. It was five days before his 61st birthday.

Mehmet Ali Agca, the Turk who shot the pope with a Browning 9mm pistol, had by then been taken to Rome police headquarters. The pope was fighting for his life in the Gemelli Hospital. It felt like no one slept that night. We kept Vatican Radio on past dawn, waiting for the grim announcement that many feared would come. Thankfully, it did not.

Four days after the shooting I went to the Santo Spirito Hospital near the Vatican to try to interview the two American women who were wounded along with the pope, Anne Odre and Rose Hall. It was 11:45 a.m. on Sunday, May 17, 1981. A young American priest outside their door told me I could not go in.

I told him that in the next 15 minutes the pope would be making a radio address from his hospital bed. He was sure to mention the wounded women and I had a portable radio. He let me in. The pope made his address in Italian, forgave Agca and said he felt close to the women who had been wounded with him. I translated the pope's words into English for the two women, who broke down and cried as he spoke.

By that time it was clear that the pope would live. But it was also clear that we were living through one of the greatest crime mysteries of all time.

Why did Agca do it, and did he act alone? It was a mystery I would follow personally for years. I covered both of Agca's trials for murder and conspiracy and talked to him for about five minutes during a break in one hearing in the mid-1980s. Agca was one of the most intriguing, enigmatic and at times frightening characters I have ever encountered. There was not enough evidence to prove a conspiracy. But still today, I do not believe he acted alone. And I hope to be alive if archives that might shed light on the shooting are opened.

But I often think of that boy who drove me on the back of his Vespa to St. Peter's Square on that hot afternoon in May more than 20 years ago. I often think of what became of him. In the end he refused to take my money.

Blood in St. Peter's Square. Writhing in pain in the popemobile moments after he was shot, May 13, 1981. Vatican photo

The unthinkable. An anxious aide cradles the wounded pope just moments after the failed assassination bid, May 13, 1981.
Vatican photo

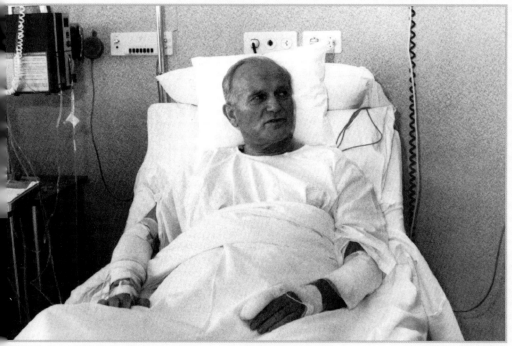

A wounded pope. Recovering in his hospital bed six days after the assassination attempt, May 19, 1981.
Vatican photo

hatch a plot to kill the pope because of his support for changes in Poland—was fascinating and highly plausible to many, but it could not be proved. On December 27, 1983, the pope visited Agca in his cell in Rome's top security Rebibbia prison. The meeting had a confessional atmosphere with a touch of the surreal. The two sat on black plastic chairs near a radiator below windows with bars. Agca, wearing a light blue sweater, jeans and running shoes, often spoke directly into the pope's left ear, the stubble of his beard almost brushing the pope's face. The pope later cut short reporters who asked if he had a clearer idea of why Agca had shot him. "What we spoke about is a secret between us. I spoke to him as I would to a brother whom I have pardoned and who enjoys my trust." Who may have been behind the assassination attempt was a secondary consideration for the pope. The emotional and physical pain of the shooting was, once again, part of the suffering he felt he had to experience for the good of the Church, his country and the world. In 1992, he underwent surgery to remove a colon tumor the size of an orange that

Forgiveness. The pope visits the would-be assassin in his Rome jail cell and pardons him, December 27, 1983.
Vatican photo

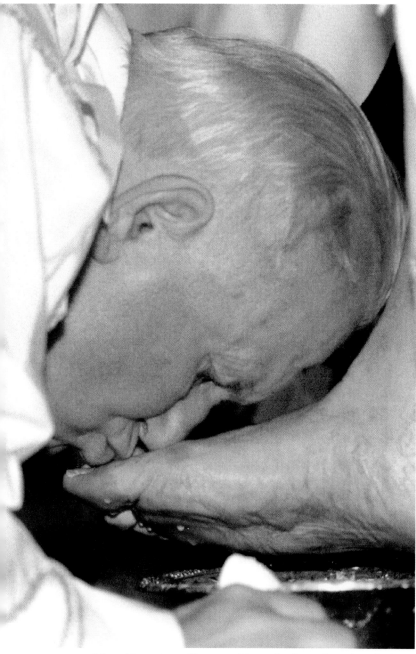

A humble gesture. The pope kisses the foot of a priest during a traditional Holy Thursday ceremony commemorating the Last Supper in St. John's in Lateran Basilica, Rome, April 13, 1995. Luciano Mellace/Reuters

the Vatican said was starting to turn malignant. In 1994, the pope slipped in his bath and broke his femur. Hurried bone replacement surgery did not fix the fracture properly, and the pope—who once skied, hiked and swam—would never walk normally again. It was about this time that signs of Parkinson's disease began to appear. As the years went by, his left arm would often tremble out of control.

As age took its toll, it became increasingly rare to hear the pope make the lengthy improvised remarks that had been a hallmark of his papacy. Yet the old spark of the preacher returned soon after his leg operation, and significantly, it was about what he saw as the need for him to suffer for the greater good. It was late May 1994, and the Vatican was clashing with the United Nations about preparations for the Conference on Population, which took place the following September in Cairo. The pope was furious over language that appeared to sanction abortion as a means of birth control in the developing world. The United Nations had declared 1994 the Year of the Family, but the pope felt the family was "under assault" and that he had to defend it. Four weeks in the hospital, he said, had made him reflect. "I understood that I have to lead the Church of Christ into this Third Millennium with prayer, with various initiatives, but I also saw that it was not enough. It had to be led (into the new millennium) with suffering, with the assassination attempt 13 years ago and with this new sacrifice," he said.

Beyond the Millennium

On December 24, 1999, the pope, dressed in resplendent robes, opened the holy door of St. Peter's Basilica to begin a year of celebrations of the new Christian Millennium. The keyword for the year was forgiveness, but the theme had been building up since the early years of his pontificate. In various addresses and gestures he had sought forgiveness for the past errors of Catholics. As an olive branch to science, he established a commission that led to the rehabilitation of Galileo. He was the first pope to preach in a Protestant church or enter a mosque. He visited Rome's synagogue, embraced its chief rabbi, Elio Toaff, and called Jews "our beloved elder brothers." He visited Germany and said that too few Catholics had stood up to Hitler. He prayed for the victims of the Holocaust at Auschwitz. In Lutheran Scandinavia he said the pain of the Reformation was caused by the faults of men on both sides.

The Word. The pope holds up the gospel at a prayer service opening the Holy Door for the Holy Year at Rome's Basilica of St. Paul, January 18, 2000. Vincenzo Pinto/Reuters

In Presov, Slovakia, he stopped to pray at a monument to 24 Calvinists killed by Catholics in 1687. He sought forgiveness from Muslims for the Crusades and from Orthodox Christians for the pain of the East–West schism. In various visits to Latin America, he lamented the injustices perpetrated by missionaries during the conquest and colonization of the New World when the cross and the sword marched hand in hand. Perhaps the most explicit words the pope used to call for an examination of conscience for the Church's misdeeds came in an internal memorandum he sent to cardinals in 1994 and which was leaked to the media. "How can we remain silent about so many forms of violence carried out in the name of faith? Wars of religion, courts of the Inquisition and other forms of violations of the rights of people?" he asked. Not surprisingly, a number of cardinals strongly opposed the pope's forgiveness proposal. Admitting past mistakes was a dangerous precedent. They balked in private, but in the end they were overruled. In one of the most poignant gestures of his entire pontificate, on March 26, 2000, the pope left a note in Jerusalem's Western Wall seeking forgiveness from Jews for the difficulties of the past. Over the objections of some of his cardinals, 2000 was not only a year of thanksgiving but also a year of atonement.

The Church After Wojtyla

The Great Jubilee Year was a time to look back. But it was also a time when many Catholics began thinking about the future. On a trip to Canada in July 2002, the pope appeared healthier than he had in months. But on his next stops in Guatemala and Mexico, the strain of travel set in and he often appeared with his head slumping to one side. The world had grown used to seeing a slower pope. The father figure had become a grandfather figure. The year 2002 also marked a time of more emotional suffering for the pope as the Catholic Church in the United States became caught up in a pedophilia scandal involving priests. It pained him tremendously, and the pope said there was no place in the priesthood for those who would harm the young. On October 16, 2002, John Paul entered the 25th year of his pontificate, the fifth longest in history. In the decade since his health problems began in 1992, the media regularly and prematurely predicted the imminent end of the Wojtyla era. In 1994, the magazine of a major world newspaper wrote a cover story about the coming end and ran profiles

Laughing with black-hooded Armenian church leaders during their visit to the Vatican, November 9, 2000.
Vincenzo Pinto/Reuters

of six possible successors among cardinals, known as "princes of the Church." One of the men in the article has since died and three have retired or turned 80, making them ineligible to enter a secret conclave to elect a new pope from among their number. The pope, by contrast, has made more than 35 additional international trips and written an array of major Church documents. There also has been much speculation that the pope could resign instead of ruling for life if he felt his health no longer allowed him to do the job. The last pope to retire willingly was Celestine V in 1294.

What will the post-Wojtyla future of the Roman Catholic Church be like? While there is much politicking ahead of a conclave, the Church believes that in the end it is the Holy Spirit that inspires the cardinals to elect the right man.

Children welcome the pope at a Vatican mass,
October 18, 1998. Paolo Cocco/Reuters

Almost as a reminder of their responsibility, the cardinals vote in secret in the Sistine Chapel before Michelangelo's awe-inspiring fresco of a stern God in the *Last Judgment*. Italians clearly want the papacy back. Some of them say the next pope should travel less and look after the central administration more, and that an Italian would be perfect for that. But many Catholics believe the next pope should not only be a non-Italian but also a non-European. A pope from Latin America, Asia or Africa, they say, would reflect the Church's universality and bolster it in areas where it is still growing and still poor. John Paul appointed more than 95 percent of the cardinals who can enter the conclave. Many of them were chosen because they are theological conservatives in the pope's own stamp. So Catholics should not expect about-faces on issues such as birth control or women priests in their lifetime. There are a number of men who have been floated as papabili, or papal candidates, to succeed John Paul. But an old Roman adage warns against trying to predict the outcome. "The man who enters the conclave as pope," it says, "leaves it as a cardinal."

Whoever he is and wherever he comes from, the next pope will have his work cut out. His every public minute will be put under the media's microscope. All his public utterances, gestures and writings will be compared to those of his predecessor. Liberals will lobby him for change. Conservatives will urge him to keep a steady hand on the tiller as he steers the "boat of St. Peter" through choppy waters. The next pope will bear the burden and responsibility of his nine formal titles: *Bishop of Rome, Vicar of Jesus Christ, Successor of the Prince of the Apostles, Supreme Pontiff of the Universal Church, Patriarch of the West, Primate of Italy, Archbishop and Metropolitan of the Roman Province, Sovereign of the State of Vatican City, Servant of the Servants of God*. As the next successor of St. Peter, the next pope will also wear the Shoes of the Fisherman. But it will be very difficult for that man to fill the shoes of Karol Wojtyla.

In His Own Words

"Do not be afraid. Open, rather open wide, the doors to Christ," from his first public address after his election on October 16, 1978, as the first non-Italian pope in more than 455 years.

"I was a laborer for four years and for me those four years of work are worth more than two doctorate degrees," addressing Rome workers in 1979.

"It's cheaper than another conclave," responding to criticism in 1979 about the cost of building a swimming pool at the papal summer residence so he could keep fit.

"The pope cannot remain a prisoner of the Vatican. I want to go to everybody…from the nomads of the steppes to the monks and nuns in their convents…. I want to cross the threshold of every home," to reporters early in his reign.

"How many popes since St. Peter have been able to ski? Answer: One!" to reporters early in his reign.

"It is not possible for us to avoid all criticism nor is it possible for us to please everyone. We are humbly convinced that God is with us in our ministry of truth, and he did not give us a spirit of timidity," during a 1979 trip to the United States.

"Is it not Christ's will that this pope, this Slav pope, should manifest at this precise moment the spiritual unity of Europe?" during his 1979 visit to Poland.

At the Western Wall, March 26, 2000. Jim Hollander/Reuters

At the Western Wall, Jerusalem, March 26, 2000

By Howard Goller

The pope took 86 steps to approach Judaism's sacred Western Wall. I counted them. They were tiny steps, and the pope walked with the aid of a cane, but in the eyes of the world he had taken a giant leap toward reconciliation—a symbolic gesture asking Jews to forgive centuries of Christian sins.

Police had closed much of Jerusalem, the heart of the Middle East conflict, to the public. As the sun bore down on that last day of only the second Holy Land trip by a pope, we witnesses, few in number, had a sense of history being made. Silence carpeted the plaza while the pope stood alone at the wall.

Then, observing a Jewish tradition, he tucked a note to God into one of the crevices. His hand trembled as he held on to one of the massive stone blocks for a moment of silent prayer and reflection. The letter, asking God's forgiveness, was typewritten on a large sheet of paper bearing the papal crest and signed by John Paul in his own hand.

"We are deeply saddened by the behavior of those who in the course of history have caused these children of yours to suffer, and, asking your forgiveness, we wish to commit ourselves to genuine brotherhood with the people of the covenant," read the message.

It remained in the wall for more than half an hour while photographers took pictures. Then an Israeli government spokesman removed the papal message and delivered it to Yad Vashem, Israel's Holocaust memorial in Jerusalem to the six million Jews killed by the Nazis.

The spokesman, Moshe Fogel, said he did not want to have it swept away by the wind. "I felt it was an historic moment and I wanted to preserve the thoughts of the pope," he said.

Under Michelangelo's ceiling. In the Sistine Chapel, January 12, 2003. Paolo Cocco/Reuters

A new Millennium. The pope looks out from his window as a crowd in St. Peter's Square celebrates with fireworks, January, 1, 2000. Vatican photo

Pope John Paul waves to the crowd at the end of his mass at
Aqueduct Raceway, New York, October 6, 1995.
Gary Hershorn/Reuters

A magnet for the faithful. A crowd packs St. Peter's Square for a beatification ceremony, September 3, 2000.
Paolo Cocco/Reuters

An historic day. His first public appearance as pope shortly after his election, October 16, 1978. Luciano Mellace/Reuters

A windy day. St. Peter's Square, September 25, 2002.
Dylan Martinez/Reuters

Admiring the view. The pope and U.S. President George W. Bush on the balcony of the pontiff's summer residence at Castel Gandolfo outside Rome, July 23, 2001.
Vatican photo

A world pulpit. Addressing the United Nations,
October 5, 1995. Gary Hershorn/Reuters

Poster-size pope. A Bulgarian worker pastes up a poster of the pope ahead of his visit to Sofia, May 21, 2002.
Dimitar Dilkoff/Reuters

Swinging the blues. The pope holds a St. Louis Blues hockey
stick given to him at a youth gathering in the United States,
January 26, 1999. Rick Wilking/Reuters

Knockin' on Heaven's Door. Bob Dylan performs for the pope in Bologna, Italy, September 27, 1997. Paolo Cocco/Reuters

Weak and drawn, the pope leaves Rome's Gemelli Hospital
after surgery to remove a colon tumor. He joked that the
hospital should be renamed Vatican II because it seemed he
spent almost as much time there as at the Vatican, 1992.
Luciano Mellace/Reuters

A different kind of popemobile. Riding in a Ferrari Mondial during a visit to the famed carmaker's plant in Maranello, Italy, June 4, 1998. Luciano Mellace/Reuters

Checking the rearview mirror as he arrives at a parish church
in Rome, November 18, 2001. Paolo Cocco/Reuters

Vatican City, April 11, 2001. Vincenzo Pinto/Reuters

Grace and grace. The pope and a young dancer during World Youth Day in Rome, August 20, 2000. Vincenzo Pinto/Reuters

Hugging Monik, three, and her one-year-old sister Zin, whose
eye can be seen between the pope's chest and hand, in
Antananarivo, Madagascar, April 29, 1989.
Luciano Mellace/Reuters

CLEMENS·X·PONT·MAX·
ANNO·IVBILEI·MDCLXXV·

A new era. Closing the Holy Door of St. Peter's
Basilica to end Millennium celebrations,
January 6, 2001. Vatican photo

Profiles in faith. Kneeling below the crucified
Christ, Stary Sacz, Poland, June 16, 1999.
Pawel Kopczynski/Reuters

Good Friday at the Colosseum, March 28, 1997.
Paolo Cocco/Reuters

A Religious Revolutionary

Sean Maguire

Henryk Lenarciak had just started a shift at the Lenin shipyard in Gdansk when a shiver of excitement coursed through the gantries and slipways. Young activists scurried from worker to worker calling a strike to demand higher wages and the reinstatement of a crane operator who had been fired. Men downed their tools, scrambled off the scaffolding that scaled the huge steel hulls and by midmorning another protest had begun in a hot Polish summer of labor unrest.

It was August 14, 1980, and the start of Solidarity, the labor movement born of hope and religious fervor that was to sweep away communist rule in Poland. It was a movement whose roots lay in the election of Pope John Paul and his triumphant return to his native Poland just 14 months earlier.

By day two of the strike, Lenarciak recalled how a huge picture of the pope was hung from the shipyard gate. Under the watchful gaze of their compatriot, inspiration and defender, the workers' protest was transformed from a dispute over labor conditions into a fight for freedom. Nine tumultuous years later Solidarity vanquished an exhausted and discredited communist regime.

"We knew what we were fighting for and we knew that eventually we had to win," said Lenarciak, who retired from the shipyard in 1987 after 37 years as a locksmith and who now ekes out a living from a pension and part-time work. "I remember that on the other side of the gate you could see half the city gathered to support us. We all prayed together."

The movement flourished on the powerful religious commitment and deep spirituality of the Polish people.

Pro-Solidarity priests said mass daily in front of the gate under the image of the pope. "Pictures of the pope were very important to us. We had deep belief and trust in our pope, and we believed that he would help us. We became more and more powerful. He gave us strength and built up our courage," said Lenarciak.

Just two weeks after the Gdansk strikes began, Lech Walesa picked up an oversized plastic pen decorated with a photograph of the pope to sign an accord with the communist government legalizing Solidarity. An unemployed yard electrician and long-time union agitator, Walesa's charisma, sense of timing and determination had catapulted him to the forefront of national unrest. The regime capitulated. They, who ruled in the name of the working class, ceded to the workers the right to organize themselves. They gave up the monopoly of power central to the survival of the Soviet system that had imposed its rule across Eastern Europe after World War Two. The dam had been breached and the shockwaves ran from Warsaw to Moscow and Beijing. Martial law, imposed in December 1981, held back the rising waters of liberty but could not stem them.

Perhaps more than anyone else, Poles had understood what the pope meant when he said at his inaugural mass in 1978, "Be not afraid." Even the apparatchiks knew they were in trouble as they watched the Vatican ceremony, the first mass ever shown by Polish state television, the tightly controlled propaganda wing of the officially atheist Communist Party. "A Pole has become pope. It's a great event for the Polish people and a great complication for us," First Secretary Edward Gierek, Poland's top-ranking communist, told his wife, foreseeing that a Polish pope would stiffen the resistance of ordinary Poles to his unelected and unloved government.

Nearly nine years after the shipyard strikes, Poles voted freely for the first time since before World War Two. In the end, Communism died quietly in Poland. The dominos fell more noisily elsewhere—Hungary, Czechoslovakia, East Germany and Romania turned away from totalitarianism, sometimes with bloodshed.

At a celebration of a decade of democracy in his native land, the pope traced the roots of those revolutions back to Solidarity's valor.

"We cannot be allowed to forget those events," the pope told Polish legislators in 1999. "They brought us not only long-sought liberty, but also contributed decisively to the collapse of the walls, which for almost half a century separated the societies and nations of our part of the continent from the free world." Solidarity was not just about people's freedom to think, believe and vote as they wished. It was about the freedom of Poles, Czechs and Hungarians to belong where they felt they belonged— in the heart of Europe, not cast behind the Iron Curtain erected by Josef Stalin to maintain the Cold War division of the continent.

Guardian Church

Solidarity traced its genesis back to the Polish pope. Tadeusz Mazowiecki, Poland's first democratically elected postwar prime minister, pitied Western observers who cannot fathom how a workers' revolt could be profoundly religious and deeply patriotic.

In Poland the Catholic Church was the guardian of the national identity, and observing the faith was an act of defiance against brutal dominance and partition of the country by Russians, Germans and Austrians for much of the last two centuries. Pilgrimage to Marian shrines and attendance at weekly mass were the minor revolts available to a subjugated people. In the drama of Polish history the pope stood as a symbol of peaceful rebellion against the "foreign" imposition of communism. "The world could not see why portraits of the pope should hang on the shipyard gates. But for us it was obvious," Mazowiecki, a Catholic intellectual who advised Solidarity, told the author in an interview.

The Gdansk strike came 14 months after the pope's first triumphant return to his homeland in June 1979. Without that trip, no opposition movement would have had the courage to emerge from the shadows. The trip gave Poles back their pride, their self-belief and the sense of common society that 30 years of communism had worn away. For nine days he traveled, praying at the tombs of St. Adalbert and St. Stanislaw and at the shrine of the Black Madonna in Czestochowa, icons of Poland's national identification with the Catholic faith. Thirteen million people, a third of the population, saw the pope in person during that ecstatic homecoming tour. He told communist authorities that peace and coexistence required an end to "all forms of economic or cultural colonialism," a clear dig at their servility before Soviet dictates. In dramatic and eloquent Polish, he forcefully defended the inalienable rights of man. Through a determined but joyful reaffirmation of the God-given worth of each human being, he transformed Poles from subjects of an alien ideology into powerful defenders of Poland's spiritual and political independence.

The visit had a practical impact, Mazowiecki recalled. The authorities demanded the Church handle the logistics, forcing the clerics to marshal a huge volunteer operation to control the crowds. It showed Poles they need not rely on the state apparatus to order every aspect of their lives.

"People found themselves in such numbers on the street, but it was all organized by ourselves and by the Church. It showed society had the power to be together. The crowds were very organized and disciplined."

Polish state television did not scan the crowds, fearful of showing their size. But it could not silence the reverberations of the words the pope uttered in Victory Square in Warsaw. He called on God to "Let your Spirit descend, and renew the face of the earth"—and with special emphasis, he repeated "this earth." The crowd knew he was referring to the ground they stood upon. It was an unmistakable call for national renaissance. It was Poland's "second baptism."

"When he said 'Let your Spirit descend,' it was like electricity ran through us all, like something was happening at that moment and something will have to follow," said Mazowiecki, who was in the crowd on that sunny Saturday in June. "Without offending the authorities he was telling them the truth."

The People Rise Up

"I had been an opposition activist for 10 years and in that time I had attracted 10 people," remembered Lech Walesa. "Out of 40 million people I could organize 10 people. But after that visit it became clear something could happen. A year later it was impossible to handle the flow of people who wanted to join us. I know the parable of the loaves and the fishes, but I think our miracle was even greater. We went from 10 people to 10 million people. People just woke up. They wanted a change and they started to believe in themselves."

The messages of religious renewal, human rights, respect for cultural heritage and spiritual tradition, the right to labor with a purpose and to govern one's own affairs would be heard again and again from the pope as he preached to tyrants, occupiers, mendacious regimes and faltering democracies later in his papacy. But the beliefs were forged and tested in Poland and found fruition in the nonviolent mass movement of Solidarity, which set an example to the world.

"There is no doubt in my mind that the changes could not have happened without the pope," said Professor Norman Davies, the preeminent foreign authority on Polish history.

The pope's visits to his homeland

BALTIC SEA

Gulf of Gdansk

RUSSIA
(Kaliningrad Region)

Gdynia
Gdansk
Koszalin
Elblag
Pelplin
Olsztyn
Elk

GERMANY

Szczecin

Lomza

KEY
🔴 **1979** *June*
🔴 **1983** *June*
🔴 **1987** *July*
🔴 **1991** *June*
🔴 **1991** *August*
🔴 **1995** *May*
🔴 **1997** *May–June*
🔴 **1999** *June*
🔴 **2002** *August*

Lichen
Notec
Bydgoszcz
Torun
Vistula
Narew

Gorzow

Bug
Drohiczyn

Gniezno
Warsaw
Siedlce

Poznan
Lowicz

Kalisz

Radom

Legnica
Warta

Wroclaw
Oder

Sandomierz
Zamosc

Czestochowa
Vistula
San

Sosnowiec
Lubaczow

Gliwice
Krakow Pope's
former archdiocese

Wadowice
Bielsko-Biala
Kalwaria Zebrzydowska

Zywiec
Ludzmierz

Zakopane

SLOVAKIA

BELARUS

UKRAINE

40 miles

*Bulletproof
"Popemobile"*

"I hope that Poland, which has belonged to Europe for centuries, will find
its proper place in the structures of the European community. Not only
will it not lose its own identity, but it will enrich the continent and the
world with its tradition."

Pope John Paul II, 2002

Source: Reuters

"There had been a long-developing economic crisis within Poland and major disaffection among the working class and society in general with the communist system. This brewed and simmered, but it was his presence and the incredible impact of his personality that set the whole process of regime disintegration in motion," said Davies, in an interview with the author. "To that extent one man can cause a revolution."

The pope was to work miracles for Poland, but what did a Polish churchman bring to the papacy? In his first moments as pope he acknowledged the challenging novelty of his election, disarming the crowd by belittling his knowledge of Italian, exploiting his winning charm and humor to strike up a rapport. "The eminent cardinals have called a new Bishop of Rome. They have called him from a far country: far, but always near through the communion of faith and in the Christian tradition," he told the faithful in St. Peter's Square on the evening of his election on October 16, 1978.

It became quickly apparent his nationality would not be a barrier. As a polyglot preacher he eroded national difference and geographic distance. His background as a philosophy professor and as a village pastor gave him broad emotional reach that cut across social classes. His training as an actor gave him rhetorical ability and dramatic presence. The prominent public roles played by Polish churchmen, stemming from the medieval era when cardinals ruled the country from the death of a king to the election of another, instilled a sense of authority and leadership. The years of calculated obstinacy in demanding Church-building permits from atheistic Party officials schooled Karol Wojtyla in the diplomatic skills he would call on later to confront the Vatican's bureaucracy and to deal with despots, dictators and dissenters.

But Wojtyla brought other, less traceable but no less valuable qualities that can loosely be defined as Polish virtues—an openness to other people, respect for national culture, quiet pride and self-confidence. His determination, self-discipline, deeply held convictions and the poetry of his sermons stemmed from his Polish intellectual and cultural heritage, said Mazowiecki.

"He faced incredible challenges after his election. He was the first non-Italian pope in more than 450 years and needed to preserve the universality of his position and at the same time stay Polish," said Mazowiecki. "That's his genius, that he managed to incorporate the best Polish traditions into his status as a universal leader."

The Patriot Pope

The pope's critics said he was just too "Polish" for the papacy, arguing that the flipside of his strength was a stubbornness typical of a nation that survived decades of subjugation. A Polish patriot, his origins sustained him and his thinking was structured by a small-town conservative upbringing in a family that embraced a strong blend of national and religious piety. His friends say the pope would not have had the strength for his global mission if he had forgotten his Polish roots while on the Vatican throne. But neither did Wojtyla wrap himself in the red and white bands of his country's flag. It was precisely because he could transcend national status that he accomplished so much for his native land. "His role in Poland was so great because his role in the world is so great," said Mazowiecki. "He's unique in Polish history."

He has been accused of giving his native land special treatment, a charge his defenders deny. "I had one chance for a longer conversation with the pope in Polish in the 1980s, and what struck me forcefully was how he looked at Poland through universal eyes. He really was looking at Poland as just one country among many," Timothy Garton Ash, an historian who has written eye-witness accounts of Solidarity and the revolutions of Eastern Europe, told me.

Wojtyla was deeply religious as a child. He was born on May 18, 1920, and his father, Karol, a noncommissioned army officer, and his mother Emilia, were both profoundly pious. The family lived in a small apartment owned by Jewish shopkeeper Yechiel Balamuth in the small town of Wadowice, in the foothills of the Beskidy mountains. It was only 35 miles away from Krakow, Poland's intellectual and cultural capital, a city that would play a vital role in Wojtyla's intellectual formation. Poland had regained its independence two years before he was born, and the spirit of the times was intensely patriotic. The Wojtyla apartment looked onto St. Mary's Church, and religious observance became part of daily life. When his mother died in 1929, both father and son found solace in prayer and pilgrimages.

Karol Wojtyla's big day. His first communion, Wadowice, Poland. Vatican photo

His father was the first of a series of strong male mentors who shaped Karol's spiritual destiny.

"We felt the charisma from him already at that time. We knew he was different from us," recalled schoolmate Eugeniusz Mroz. "He had a tremendously profound religious belief." He remembered Lolek, the Polish nickname for Karol, as a brilliant student with a gift for languages. He was fluent in Latin, Greek and German by the time he graduated from high school. He was also an enthusiastic sportsman, a lover of hill-walking, skiing and soccer, where his friends remember his wide frame making him useful between the goalposts. His other great passion was the theater.

"He had an extraordinary memory and a beautiful silvery voice," remembered Mroz. "He had enormous potential as an actor. That was his dream then." Wojtyla starred in local productions of Athenian dramas and 19th-century works by dramatists from the Polish Romantic tradition, whose

With his father.
East News

he did so as a man who endured terror and conflict and who had survived an aerial bombardment. When he prayed for an end to tyranny, he recalled escaping a Gestapo dragnet, living on starvation rations and walking through streets lined with posters naming men arbitrarily executed by Germans to punish acts of resistance. When he prayed for the victims of the Holocaust, he remembered the disappearance of his own Jewish friends from Wadowice and the extermination of the thriving Jewish community in Krakow. When he spoke of the dignity of labor, he remembered the four years of backbreaking work

As a young priest. The young Father Karol Wojtyla in the 1940s. Vatican photo

The skiing priest.
East News

work had sustained the hopes for nationhood during occupation. He moved to Krakow in 1938 to study the Polish language, continuing his own poetic and dramatic writing and immersing himself in theatrical activity. Before his second year of studies could begin, Germany and Russia invaded Poland in September 1939. World War Two had begun.

War, his father's death and the struggle between his theatrical and his religious vocation marked Wojtyla's early twenties. As pope, when he prayed for the lonely, he remembered the emptiness that surrounded him when his father died in 1941, leaving him without a single close relative before he was 21. When he prayed for world peace, shoveling rocks and lugging buckets of lime in a quarry and chemicals plant, jobs arranged by friends to spare him expulsion to forced labor in German concentration camps.

"He often worked at night, to give himself time to think and pray," said Edward Goerlich, an engineer who remembers talking about science to the curious Wojtyla at the chemicals plant. "We had lots of discussions, and one day he came to me and told me he had decided to become a priest."

The decision did not shock Halina Kwiatkowska, who grew up alongside Lolek in Wadowice and was part of a wartime recital group in Krakow. Called the Rhapsodic Theater, it was named after the mythical Rhapsodes who wandered from village to village comforting the spirits of people tormented by war. "We were resisting with the word, not the gun," recalled Kwiatkowska. Performances, if discovered by the Germans, would have been punished by death. Audiences could not applaud for fear of discovery. The recitals were of 19th-century historical and mystical dramas, often imbued with a religious subtext. For Wojtyla, culture and history had become weapons vital to sustaining a nation's soul. But for his own soul, he had to go further. Despite the passionate efforts of his theatrical mentor, Mieczyslaw Kotlarczyk, to dissuade him, Karol walked to the 17th-century archbishop's residence in August 1942 and asked to be admitted to the underground seminary. "He'd have made a wonderful actor but I don't regret that he didn't make that choice," said Kwiatkowska, now a professional actress. "We'd have missed out on a great pope."

Ten days after he was ordained in 1946, Wojtyla performed his first baptism as a priest, welcoming Kwiatkowska's daughter Monika into the Catholic Church. Days later he left his beloved Poland for the first time, moving to Rome to continue his theological studies. When he returned two years later, Poland was in the icy grip of hard-line communist rule.

Intelligent Resistance

Early in his priesthood Wojtyla established a pattern of intelligence, approachability and innovation while keeping a watchful eye on tradition. It was a pattern that would later help him steer the Church. He combined pastoral care for ordinary Catholics struggling to keep

Pope Paul VI places the red berretta on Archbishop Karol Wojtyla to make him a cardinal, June 26, 1967.
Vatican photo

their faith amid repression with a formidable intellectual output, lecturing on theology while writing scores of essays, poems and dramas for local publication, mainly under pseudonyms. He defied stereotypes of the intellectual cleric or the church bureaucrat. He began marriage preparation classes that did not shy from issues of sexuality, wrote a guidebook on responsible love and started discussion forums with scientists, artists, teachers and doctors. As priest, he was ostensibly nonpolitical, but his work wrapped the Church around all aspects of people's lives, buffering them from the dehumanizing effects of Stalinist strictures.

For Wojtyla, the most personally valuable initiative of the postwar years was the development of a circle of young friends, mainly students, who became his intellectual challengers, discussion partners, camping companions and loyal allies. Together the group hiked, talked and kayaked in the Polish mountains and lakes. He presided at the

A Polish pope. Before the cameras just days after his election, 1978. Mal Langsdon/Reuters

wife Maria was among the original group, which still keeps close contact with the man they addressed as "Wujek" (Uncle). "We were something between friends, pupils and family for him," said Rybicki. "It was all informal and of course highly illegal."

The communists had banned the clergy from leading youth groups and saying mass outside churches. Across the Eastern Bloc religion was reviled as a rival to the "higher truth" of communism. Clergy were harassed and jailed and the lives of worshippers made miserable. Catholicism was too strong in Poland to be repressed totally, but the regime closed seminaries, imprisoned priests, censored publications and sent Wyszynski into internal exile for three years. Wojtyla led his hiking group by disguising himself in civilian clothes. He was drawing on the pattern of intelligent resistance and quiet moral affirmation against evil that he had begun in wartime Krakow.

As bishop, archbishop and cardinal, Wojtyla did not seek confrontation with the regime but drew lines over which it should not step. As his rank and stature within the Polish Church increased, so did his political sophistication. The government had pressed for him to be appointed archbishop of Krakow in 1963 instead of others thought to be more stubborn. It was soon regretting its mistake. Wojtyla resisted successfully when the authorities tried to seize seminary buildings, and he fought to reopen the Theological Faculty in Krakow's Jagiellonian University, shut down by the communists in 1954. To protest against the government's refusal to allow a church in the vast, newly built working-class suburb of Nowa Huta, he celebrated Christmas midnight mass every year outdoors in the freezing cold. The church was finally built and dedicated in 1977.

Early in his career Wojtyla recognized the moral damage inflicted on individuals by a loss of liberty, whether under Nazism or communism. But the critical steps forward were his experience of Vatican II, the Church's great modernizing council in the early 1960s, and his implementation of its teachings in his own diocese. It was no longer sufficient for the Church to defend itself; freedom must be understood more broadly. "That leap from talking about the rights of the Church or the rights of Christians to talking about universal human rights was absolutely crucial," said Garton Ash. It paved the way for the grand alliance of 1980 between the secular left, intellectuals, workers and the Church that made Solidarity happen.

marriage of many of the members of the "milieu" and was on their treasured annual kayak trip in 1958 when he was told he had become the youngest bishop in Poland. He hurried to Warsaw, borrowed a cassock to meet Cardinal Stefan Wyszynski, the Polish primate, and then returned to the lakes. He would kayak every year with his milieu until his election as pope. The group helped him learn more about ordinary life and its challenges. Wojtyla was no ivory-tower churchman.

"He was resistant to small disasters, such as the capsizing of a kayak or tiring days," said Stanislaw Rybicki, who with his

The Role of Gorbachev

Solidarity could not have happened without the Polish pope. Nor could it have succeeded in restoring democracy in Poland if other pieces of the puzzle had not fallen into place.

The stout support of the United States, the economic collapse of the Soviet bloc and the stubbornness of ordinary Poles were all part of the jigsaw. Yet many historians say it was the elevation of Mikhail Gorbachev to the top of the Soviet Communist Party in 1985 that permitted far-reaching change in Eastern Europe. Under Gorbachev, the Russian bear sheathed its claws, declaring it would no longer use force to maintain communism in its sphere of influence. The Brezhnev doctrine of intervention was over. But Gorbachev gives the pope the credit for stimulating the revolutions of 1989 and the collapse of the Soviet Union in 1991. "Everything that happened in Eastern Europe in these last few years would have been impossible without the presence of this pope," Gorbachev wrote in 1992, after his fall from power. Without Solidarity and the pope, Gorbachev's foreign policy would not have been so challenged. "The fact that Gorbachev realized as soon as he came to power that he had to radically revise Soviet–East Europe policy was in large measure because Poland had not been 'normalized'," said Garton Ash.

Former Polish leader General Wojciech Jaruzelski, who imposed martial law in 1981 in a vain attempt to stop Solidarity, was more complimentary about Gorbachev. He cited an old Russian proverb that says water does not run beneath a stone, a metaphor for the immobility of the Kremlin old guard. "It was Gorbachev who finally lifted the stone," the old Polish general said. Jaruzelski, keen to secure what credit he can from history, said he played a role in helping the pope and Gorbachev understand they were no threat to each other.

"Already in 1985, I was telling Gorbachev that he should think differently about the pope, that he was a man of peace, of a new social knowledge, and a fellow Slav who wants good relations with Russia," Jaruzelski said in an interview with the author. "And I told the pope that Gorbachev is modern, he wants reforms. The pope listened attentively and asked questions."

The leader of the officially atheist nuclear superpower and the head of a religion virulently opposed to communism

Hugging a Polish child, Poland, 1979.
Chris Niedenthal/FORUM

finally met in December 1989 at the Vatican. Gorbachev called the encounter "truly extraordinary"; the pope called it "singularly meaningful: a sign of the times." It ended the tumultuous battle between the Vatican and Soviet ideologues over who spoke the higher truth to mankind. The meeting concluded decades of harsh anti-Vatican Soviet propaganda and stood as a papal endorsement of Gorbachev's *perestroika* (restructuring) efforts.

A third pilgrimage to Krakow, Poland, 1987.
Chris Niedenthal/FORUM

domineering past and to end the Cold War were vital in the fall of the Iron Curtain and the reunification of Europe, a central papal aspiration. But many historians say that while the pope was a master of circumstance, Gorbachev was its victim. Gorbachev wanted to reform communism, not end it. He wanted to keep the Soviet Union together, not let its reluctant constituents, like overwhelmingly Catholic Lithuania, flee into independence as they did in 1991.

"The pope, without firing a shot, destroyed the authority of the Soviet system. He made people see it was based not on their interests or on their support but on brute force. And then you got this extraordinary general secretary (Gorbachev) who didn't really want to use brute force," said Professor Davies. "And lo and behold the whole thing just collapsed, the Soviet system just died on its feet."

Some historians debate the extent of the pope's role in bringing down communism outside Poland and spreading democracy across Europe. But Davies believed the pope's "exemplary quality" was significant in the tumbling of governments. The events he inspired in Poland, by pricking the bubble of communist invincibility, helped to deflate

Gorbachev described the pope as an ally, not an enemy, and as someone whose support the Soviet leader needed to force through change. He promised a law to allow freedom of conscience, presaging a new dawn for harshly repressed religions across the old Soviet bloc. For the pope, it was a high point in the struggle for religious and personal freedoms.

The pope often described Gorbachev as "a providential man," someone who had the right beliefs at the right place and time to change the fate of nations. Gorbachev's attempts to modernize the Soviet Union, to shake off its

During a trip to Poland, the pope stands under a Solidarity banner, 1983. Vatican photo

regimes far from his homeland, said Davies. Garton Ash described Poland as the "icebreaker." But even if his success was confined to Poland, that would be a monumental achievement.

I Hate to Leave You

George Weigel, author of the highly acclaimed papal biography *Witness to Hope*, believes toppling communism was one of the great accomplishments of one of history's great popes. It was, Weigel wrote in 1999, the "achievement of a courageous pastor, determined to speak truth to power and convinced that the word of truth, spoken clearly and forcefully enough, is the most effective tool against the tyranny of totalitarianism."

The pope's native land is now a stable democracy, which by joining NATO and the European Union is at the forefront of efforts to bridge Europe's historic divides. It is an increasingly prosperous nation. But it is also increasingly secular. Church attendance has fallen, and the political power of the clergy and the respect accorded to priests have diminished. The new freedoms mean worship is no longer a patriotic act in Poland. Some suggest Poles have disappointed the pope. He has wagged his finger at them for succumbing to the materialism, moral indifference and selfishness of uncaring capitalism. But wayward children still love their fathers. All of the pope's homecomings, even those after the fall of communism, were festivals of mutual devotion. Wherever he went a sea of faces was etched with tears and thousands of voices were raised in song and prayer. It was the coming together of a people and a pope who endured a common struggle and prevailed.

"I hate to leave you," were the pope's last words to the crowd before he flew from Krakow airport in August 2002. A ray of sun fought through the clouds as the plane dipped towards his beloved mountains. He was gone.

In His Own Words

"The military regime has existed since December, the Madonna of Czestochowa, for 600 years," telling Polish pilgrims to keep the faith after the declaration of martial law in 1981.

"To remember Hiroshima is to abhor war," in 1981 while visiting the site of the world's first nuclear wartime blast.

"Things really have to change here," delivering a public lecture on inequality to a stony faced President Jean-Claude Duvalier in Haiti during a trip there in 1983.

"When I speak out in defense of human rights, above all about religious freedom, I do not accuse the authorities of any country. If, at times, certain authorities feel attacked, it is perhaps because they feel guilty," speaking to aides after delivering a strong speech in defense of refugees following a visit to a refugee camp in Thailand in 1984.

"It's a wonder to me too," responding to a reporter who asked him how he managed not to feel exhausted after a trip to Latin America in 1985.

"Christians and Muslims—generally we have understood each other badly. Sometimes in the past we have opposed each other and even exhausted ourselves in polemics and wars. I believe that God is calling us today to change our old habits," during a visit to Casablanca, Morocco, in 1985.

"You are our dearly beloved brothers, and in a certain way it could be said that you are our elder brothers," addressing Jews during his historic visit to Rome's synagogue in 1986.

With his mentor. Embracing Cardinal Stefan Wyszynski, who
was his superior in Poland, May 16, 1979.
Vatican photo

The man of steel and the man in white. The pope and Polish leader General Wojciech Jaruzelski review the troops, 1987.
Santiago Lyon/Reuters

Electrifying a Nation

By David Storey

The election of Karol Wojtyla, former archbishop of Krakow, as pope on October 16, 1978, electrified the repressed people of his homeland who had lived under Nazism and communism for nearly four decades. As Reuters correspondent in Warsaw, I reported on two trips Pope John Paul made to his homeland and saw at first hand the light of hope and courage he ignited in his people's hearts.

John Paul never left behind the humanity, the humor, the compassion of Karol Wojtyla, the philosopher, teacher and actor who had labored in a quarry and worked in the underground church while Nazi Germany savaged his country.

Handsome and avuncular, the pope swept into his homeland in the summer of 1979 combining the allure of a rock star with the power of an avenging angel. About 13 million of his fellow Poles crowded into squares, meadows and parks to see him. Although he preached patience and sacrifice, Poles were galvanized by his message to believe in themselves and in the power of Christ.

Unlike their distant and shifty Communist rulers, Poles found in the pope's presence a directness and approachability. Even those who could hardly make out the tall figure in his white and gold robes as they stood in a million-strong throng felt personally touched, whether in the meadows outside Krakow or the flat paved acres of Warsaw's central Victory Square.

Two decades later, Lech Walesa, the Gdansk dockyard electrician who led Solidarity and became president of Poland, assessed the pope's impact. "Communism ended because it was a bad system. I would, however, estimate the Holy Father's input in its demise at about 50 percent, Solidarity's maybe 30 percent." Before Wojtyla's election, Walesa struggled to rally dozens behind his calls for freedom. Afterwards, he said, he had millions behind that cause.

The flame stayed alight in Poland even after the army leader General Wojciech Jaruzelski declared martial law in a snowy night on December 13, 1981, in a desperate attempt to save communist control. Pope John Paul came back in 1983 to restore the faith of his people in their ultimate liberation, in the power of their own culture and history and their belief in the truth.

Once again the country went on the move. People reaffirmed the helplessness of the communist rulers and police to control their thoughts and hopes. In Krakow, just outside the medieval city center, I sat up through the night in a hotel room overlooking the path to the meadows where the pope was to speak the next day. All night there was an endless flow of people. They walked to the gentle thump of heavy drums, sometimes raising wavering voices in hymns. It was a constant shuffle and rustle of tens of thousands on the march.

Through the darkness and the subdued sounds radiated an almost palpable excitement. At dawn the sun rose on one of the biggest crowds assembled in human history. It parted to allow a papal procession to the altar in the middle of the fields. I rode on an open truck ahead of the pope's vehicle, past faces of young girls, youths, men and women, all turned to catch the magic, some cheeks glistening with tears, some arms raised with the two-fingered V-sign of Solidarity. Everywhere, anticipation.

At his stop in Czestochowa, half a million gathered beneath the ramparts of the monastery, one of Poland's holiest shrines. Chanting and singing, they would not let him speak, calling "The pope with us" and "Closer to us, closer to us." In a classic piece of Karol Wojtyla theatricality, he said: "I am coming closer" and moved down towards the throng with an aide struggling to bring the microphone. The crowd was delighted and it stilled them.

After a day hopping by helicopter from open-air masses to meetings with his bishops and informal sessions with his countrymen, the pope returned hours late to the monastery. Throngs waited in the dark to catch a glimpse of him. Suddenly, on a high terrace on the battlements a spotlight flashed on and there he was, a scarlet cape over his shoulders, energized by the sea of people singing for him among the trees and on the lawns below the dark walls. He seemed to float above the crowd, inexhaustible, untouchable.

Pictures of the formal meeting between the pope and Jaruzelski in Warsaw revealed the gulf between the uniformed agent doing what Poles believed was the bidding of Moscow and the messenger of national hope, peace and forgiveness. On one side was the stiff figure of the balding general, medal ribbons across his chest and dark glasses hiding his eyes.

By contrast, the pope, in white robes, relaxed and confident, delivered a simple message—that the rebuilding of society shattered by the military crackdown could only start by reinstating the social accords struck with the now-banned Solidarity in 1980. It was the voice of the people.

Through all his visits, including his latest in 2002, when he said goodbye to his compatriots through tears, the essential message to his adoring fellow Poles remained unflinching and unchanged: Be not afraid and live in truth.

Lech Walesa with one of his daughters in Gdansk, November 1980. Chris Niedenthal/FORUM

Kneeling before the son of Polish soil. Lech Walesa and his wife Danuta at a papal mass in Gdansk, Poland, June 12, 1987. Luciano Mellace/Reuters

Striking shipyard workers hang a portrait of the pope on a
shipyard gate in Gdansk. Leszek Wdowinski/FORUM

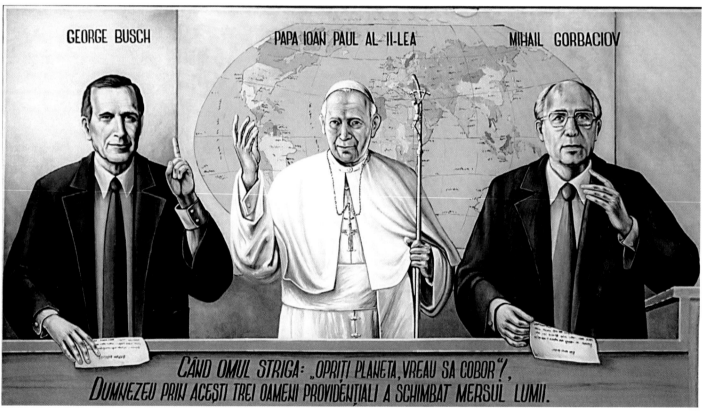

GEORGE BUSCH

PAPA IOAN PAUL AL II-LEA

MIHAIL GORBACIOV

CÂND OMUL STRIGĂ: „OPRIȚI PLANETA, VREAU SĂ COBOR",
DUMNEZEU PRIN ACEȘTI TREI OAMENI PROVIDENȚIALI A SCHIMBAT MERSUL LUMII.

Men who changed the world. Portraits of U.S. President
George H. W. Bush, the pope, and Soviet leader Mikhail
Gorbachev in a Romanian Orthodox church in the village of
Petresti before the pope's visit to the country,
August 26, 2001. Bogdan Cristel/Reuters

The pope and Soviet leader Mikhail Gorbachev at their historic first meeting at the Vatican, December 1, 1989.
Luciano Mellace/Reuters

Cold War warriors. The pope with U.S. President Ronald
Reagan at the Vatican, June 6, 1987. Vatican photo

With U.S. President George H. W. Bush at the Vatican,
November 8, 1991. Rick Wilking/Reuters

A reunited Germany. The pope and Chancellor Helmut Kohl
at Berlin's famous Brandenburg Gate, June 23, 1996.
Reinhard Krause/Reuters

Snapshots of the boss. Bishops turned photographers during the pope's visit to Wroclaw, Poland, May 31, 1997.
Leszek Wdowinski/Reuters

With Polish youngsters at his summer residence,
August 7, 2002. Dylan Martinez/Reuters

There he is! Polish children point to a papal helicopter as it
arrives in Radzymin, Poland, June 13, 1999.
Vincenzo Pinto/Reuters

Nuns wave to the pope in Krakow, Poland, August 18, 2002.
Jerry Lampen/Reuters

Reviewing a Polish military guard of honor, Krakow, Poland, August 16, 2002. Vincenzo Pinto/Reuters

The way they were. The pope shares a meal and memories
with old school friends, Krakow, Poland, August 18, 2002.
Vatican photo

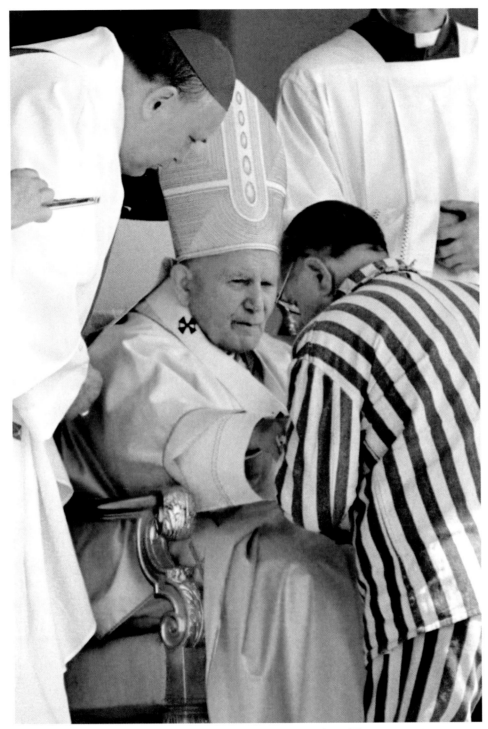

With a concentration camp survivor. The pope greets
Zbigniew Mazurek, wearing inmate's uniform, recalling his
days in the Gross-Rosen camp during World War Two,
Legnica, Poland, June 2, 1997. Jerry Lampen/Reuters

A dutiful son. Too weak to leave his popemobile, the pope
stops to pray at the graves of his parents at Krakow cemetery,
August 18, 2002. Vincenzo Pinto/Reuters

Krakow, Poland. It was the pope's ninth papal visit to his homeland, August 17, 2002. Vincenzo Pinto/Reuters

Under the Polish eagle. Speaking to politicians in Warsaw,
June 11, 1999. Jerry Lampen/Reuters

On the Road
with Pope John Paul

Philip Pullella

Lech Rynkiewicz counts kilometers and tallies days, hours and minutes. He calculates the relationship between those kilometers to the distance between the earth and the moon and the circumference of the globe. He is neither an astronomer nor a cartographer, but a Polish priest who keeps track of Pope John Paul's travels for Vatican Radio. Each time the pope returns from a trip outside the Vatican walls, Rynkiewicz sits in his small office and updates his log. When the pope began the 25th year of his pontificate on October 16, 2002, he had traveled a total of 1,237,584 kilometers, or 769,163 miles. This, Father Rynkiewicz's statistics show, is some 30 times the circumference of the globe and more than three times the distance between the earth and the moon. By the time he had marked his 24th anniversary, the pope had been outside the Vatican for 946 days, 17 hours and five minutes, equivalent to about 11 percent of his papacy. He had made 142 trips in Italy and visited 129 different countries on 98 foreign tours. This is not including the hundreds of visits to parishes, institutions and churches in the Rome area.

To compare Pope John Paul to his predecessors is like comparing Christopher Columbus to a couch potato. Three pontiffs in the late 19th and early 20th centuries—Leo XIII, Pius X and Benedict XV—never ventured outside the Vatican because of political turmoil in Italy between 1870 and 1929. Pius XII, who reigned from 1939 to 1958, left Rome only to go to the papal summer residence just south of the Italian capital. Pope John XXIII made just two trips, both of them in Italy, during his years on the papal throne from 1958 to 1963. Pope Paul VI began international travel in 1964, a year after his election, but made only nine trips in 15 years. Before Paul VI, no pope had left Italy since Pius VII was forced into exile at Fontainebleau by Napoleon in 1812.

For those who knew Karol Wojtyla before his election as pope in 1978, his wanderlust came as no surprise. As a priest in Poland, he would get on a bicycle and go visit his parishioners. When he wanted to discuss problems with his young students, he would organize trips to the Tatra Mountains or the lakes of northern Poland so they could walk and talk, hike and talk, canoe and talk. John Paul decided early on to leave his mark on the papacy more than the papacy would leave its mark on him. Getting out of the Vatican, which he more than once likened to a jail, would help him do just that. "You have to know that prison to appreciate this freedom," he told reporters who had tracked him down to a tiny village in the Dolomite mountains of northern Italy during the first "private" vacation a pope had taken in modern times. Early in his pontificate, the pope encountered much resistance to his travel plans in the Vatican's often-staid bureaucracy, known as the curia. Many thought that an average of four long trips a year was just too much. The pope told the Italian Catholic writer Gian Franco Svidercoschi in 1989 that when he was elected he had no idea that he would travel so much. "But something new was taking shape. On the one hand there was my increasingly convinced desire to make them [trips] and on the other hand the desire of local churches to host visits increased," he said.

Pilgrim's Progress

Journalists quickly came up with some catchy titles for the traveling pontiff. "God's Globetrotter" and the "Pilgrim Pope" were among them. For John Paul, however, the travels were a teaching tool, an extension of his message and his authority, and of the Vatican's foreign policy. Before popes began traveling, the messages and teachings that emanated from the confines of the Vatican filtered down to the faithful through layers of Catholic hierarchy to creaky wooden pulpits where parish priests would preach about them. Instead, the world became John Paul's pulpit. There he was preaching the "sermon on the mound" in New York's Yankee Stadium, telling Americans they could not neglect their poor. There he was in Vienna preaching tolerance in the same square where Adolf Hitler addressed the adoring masses before the start of World War Two. There he was on his knees at Auschwitz praying for the Jewish victims of the Holocaust. There he was spoon-feeding the dying in Mother Teresa's Kaligat hospice in the slums of Calcutta. There he was on the Senegalese island of Goree, standing at the narrow, stone loading bay where millions of Africans had been herded onto slave ships. "From this African sanctuary of black pain, we implore forgiveness from Heaven," he said at Goree. There he was at ground zero in Hiroshima appealing, "To remember Hiroshima is to abhor war."

Papal messages, once distant and complicated, hit home with unexpected clarity precisely because they were delivered in places where people lived, worked and died. The place was part of the message. In several countries, including Poland and the Philippines, papal visits gathered the largest crowds in the nations' histories, far outstripping military parades, liberation commemorations and state funerals. And yet many in the crowds, whether they were in San Salvador or San Francisco, Paris or Panama City, often told reporters the same thing: "I felt like he was speaking only to me, like it was just the two of us." Thus did the media bestow another title on the pope—"The Great Communicator." It fit his ability to preach to the millions while hitting the heart of an individual with the precision of a spiritual sniper.

All Work, No Play

Although elected for life, the pope traveled and stumped as if he were running for office. His pace in the early days of his papacy, when he sometimes would make more than 10 speeches in a day, was so punishing that Vatican clerics and journalists half his age who accompanied him would return to Rome exhausted. He almost never toured the places most people go to see in New York, Paris, Mexico City or Bangkok. But he often drew on their symbolic power to add force to his message. He stood in lower Manhattan's Battery Park in the shadow of the Statue of Liberty and urged Americans never to forget their immigrant culture or close their doors to newcomers. In some places such as the United States, where some Catholics were in open dissent, travel was a two-edged sword. The pope talked, but listeners talked back. At a 1987 meeting in Los Angeles, Cardinal Joseph Bernardin told the pope in public that he just did not understand the spirit of freethinking Americans. "It is important to know that many Americans, given the freedom that they have enjoyed for more than two centuries, almost instinctively react negatively when they are told that they must do something," Bernardin said. The pope responded: "It is sometimes claimed that dissent is totally compatible with being a good Catholic and poses no obstacle to the reception of the sacraments. This is a grave error. Dissent is dissent and as such may not be proposed or received on an equal footing with the Church's authentic teaching." There he was on someone else's turf reminding them of the rules, his rules.

Papal Q&A at 33,000 Feet

Before John Paul, regular papal encounters with the media were practically nonexistent. He changed this by talking to reporters who accompanied him on his travels. The pope's international flights quickly became precious opportunities because they were the only occasions reporters had to put questions directly to the leader of one billion Roman Catholics. During early trips, they were total chaos. The pope would appear in the rear section of the plane where the 50 or so reporters traveled. He would walk down one aisle of the wide-bodied aircraft and up the other, taking question after question. Food trays would fly as reporters climbed over seats to hear as much as possible. Cabin assistants were not amused. Sometimes, the pope's aides were forced to act like bouncers protecting a rock star, grabbing a reporter by the lapels and hurling him to the side. On one trip, when all the journalists had rushed over to one aisle of the aircraft to hear the pope, the pilot ordered them to return to their seats because the plane was being thrown off balance. Another news conference in the heavens was cut short by turbulence. The pope took it all in his stride, often laughing at the unseemly scrum around him.

The pope believed it was important to have individual contact with each reporter. He realized early on that the media would play an important role in his pontificate and often spoke of the responsibility of the journalist. "No one can be a [journalist] for one's own exclusive purpose," he once told reporters. "Your profession requires a constant and pressing effort to tune in to the wavelength of reality and also requires a balanced discernment that clearly safeguards the rights of truth and the duties toward society." Sister Mary Ann Walsh, an American nun who worked as a reporter in Rome in the early 1980s, recalled a revealing episode. "I was seated in the front of the reporters' section reading when suddenly this white sleeve was in front of my eyes. The pope had come back to our section earlier than expected and was reaching out to shake hands. I tried to get up but was kept in place by my seatbelt. I fumbled for a notebook and realized with frustration that a moment I had looked forward to—a rare chance to ask the pope a question on the record—was slipping away fast. The pope quickly assessed the situation,

(continued on page 86)

A weary traveler. The pope returns from a trip, Rome, June 21, 1998. Paolo Cocco/Reuters

Puddles in Paradise

By Luciano Mellace

On November 11, 1986, we arrived in Suva, Fiji, one stop on Pope John Paul's swing through the South Pacific. A tropical storm had passed over the islands, leaving the airport pockmarked with puddles. I noticed that the organizers had scrambled to find a straw mat to lay on the tarmac so the pope could kiss the ground without getting his cassock wet. There we were on an island associated with sun and beaches.

The entire place was dripping after the storm, and I knew I had to capture the religion but also the rain. As the organizers found a relatively dry spot among the puddles to position the mat, I positioned myself to take the picture I wanted. I saw it in my mind even before pushing the shutter. I closed in with a long lens and concentrated on a puddle of water just in front of the pope's mat. When the pope was reflected in the water, I lifted the lens to get the mirror image.

That afternoon, I was sending the picture to Reuters headquarters in London via an old-style rotating drum transmitter, a crude precursor to today's scanners. The pope's spokesman, Joaquin Navarro-Valls, walked into the press center by chance and, when he saw the picture, asked me to make a copy for him.

The next day on the plane taking us to New Zealand, the next stop on the tour, Navarro-Valls took the print up to the plane's front section, where the pope was sitting. He returned about 10 minutes later with the print signed by the pope with his formal title in Latin: Joannes Paulus PP II. He said it brought a smile to the pope's face.

Some of my photographer colleagues were envious. They asked if the pope could sign some of their pictures, but to no avail. In my career covering five popes, it was the picture that gave me the most satisfaction. It is now framed on my wall at home.

Pope John Paul reflected in a pool of water as he kisses the ground upon landing at Nausori Airport in Suva, Fiji, November 21, 1986. Luciano Mellace/Reuters

Reaching out. Oropa, Italy, July 16, 1989.
Luciano Mellace/Reuters

smiled and said 'I'll be back.' I thought all was lost until a while later, on his way back to his seat, he stopped in front of me as promised and I got my question in."

The pope made about four trips a year, so questions aboard the plane usually centered on either the country or region where he was headed or a world event that had occurred since his last trip. Reporters would regularly "gang up" on the pope, asking him the same question time and again, or a variation of it, hoping to extract something on a delicate matter that he preferred to avoid. In later years, the pope gave in to aides and airline personnel who wanted to rein in the confusion. A crude, centralized sound system was devised. The pope stood at the front of the rear section and took just a few questions from reporters who had been ordered to stay in their seats. It was perhaps more efficient, yet the spark was gone and so was the fun. But at times one could see the communicator's gleam in his eye, the desire to return to individual contact and the unholy chaos at 33,000 feet.

The reign of the traveling pope

In the first 24 years of his reign, Pope John Paul II has become the most traveled pontiff in history, covering nearly 800,000 miles on trips in Italy and abroad, equivalent to about 30 times the circumference of the earth

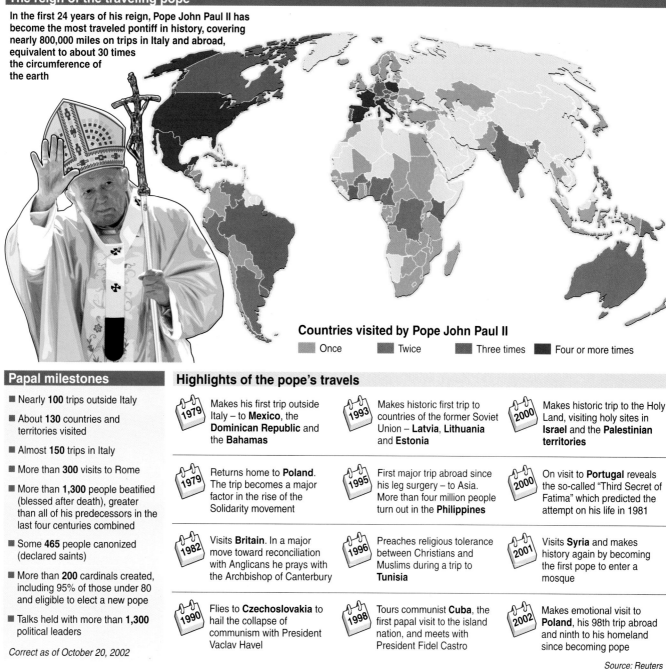

Countries visited by Pope John Paul II

Once   Twice   Three times   Four or more times

Papal milestones

- Nearly **100** trips outside Italy
- About **130** countries and territories visited
- Almost **150** trips in Italy
- More than **300** visits to Rome
- More than **1,300** people beatified (blessed after death), greater than all of his predecessors in the last four centuries combined
- Some **465** people canonized (declared saints)
- More than **200** cardinals created, including 95% of those under 80 and eligible to elect a new pope
- Talks held with more than **1,300** political leaders

Correct as of October 20, 2002

Highlights of the pope's travels

1979 Makes his first trip outside Italy – to **Mexico**, the **Dominican Republic** and the **Bahamas**

1993 Makes historic first trip to countries of the former Soviet Union – **Latvia**, **Lithuania** and **Estonia**

2000 Makes historic trip to the Holy Land, visiting holy sites in **Israel** and the **Palestinian territories**

1979 Returns home to **Poland**. The trip becomes a major factor in the rise of the Solidarity movement

1995 First major trip abroad since his leg surgery – to Asia. More than four million people turn out in the **Philippines**

2000 On visit to **Portugal** reveals the so-called "Third Secret of Fatima" which predicted the attempt on his life in 1981

1982 Visits **Britain**. In a major move toward reconciliation with Anglicans he prays with the Archbishop of Canterbury

1996 Preaches religious tolerance between Christians and Muslims during a trip to **Tunisia**

2001 Visits **Syria** and makes history again by becoming the first pope to enter a mosque

1990 Flies to **Czechoslovakia** to hail the collapse of communism with President Vaclav Havel

1998 Tours communist **Cuba**, the first papal visit to the island nation, and meets with President Fidel Castro

2002 Makes emotional visit to **Poland**, his 98th trip abroad and ninth to his homeland since becoming pope

Source: Reuters

With Mother Teresa outside her home for the dying, Calcutta, India, February 3, 1986. Luciano Mellace/Reuters

A Kiss Is Not Just a Kiss

When the pope landed, the world saw the gesture that became one of his trademarks—kissing the ground. It was sometimes loaded with emotional and political significance, such as the kiss at Cologne airport when he first visited Germany in 1980. Here was a pope kissing the soil of the country that had tried to wipe out his native Poland in a war that had ended only 35 years before. Even German and Polish bishops had chilly relations, with some Germans questioning the validity of the postwar border. With one kiss of the tarmac at a German airport, the pope sent a message to everyone, including his own bishops: "The war ended a long time ago. Let's move on."

A papal kiss of disputed ground could be more than a kiss; it could have enormous political weight. One place the pope did not kiss the ground was East Timor in 1989 when the territory was still under Indonesian rule. Cardinal Roberto Tucci, who was the chief organizer of papal trips for 20 years, recalled how the pope handled the delicate situation. "The [Indonesian] generals insisted that the pope should not recognize East Timor as an independent state and the pope had no intention to do so at the time. He merely wanted East Timorese to have their human rights, their religion and their language and culture respected. Since the situation was difficult, it was arranged beforehand that Bishop Carlos Belo would hold a large crucifix and the pope would kiss it instead of the ground at the airport. When we arrived I got off the plane first and saw there was no crucifix on the tarmac. Belo told me that the authorities had confiscated it. Later, when the pope was preparing for mass, he called me into the sacristy and he told me to place a crucifix on a cushion on the ground in front of the altar. When the pope arrived at the altar to begin the mass, he bent to kiss the crucifix, which was on the ground. So it went badly for the Indonesian generals."

Masses and Critical Mass

Belo won the Nobel Peace Prize in 1996 and East Timor achieved independence in 2002. It was just one of the places that the pope visited in times when social revolutions were gathering critical mass, where his presence became a catalyst for change. The papal effect was not limited to Poland. It left its mark elsewhere too. In 1981 the pope visited the Philippines, Asia's only predominantly Catholic country. The dictator Ferdinand Marcos and his wife Imelda, Asia's answer to Argentina's Evita Peron, were furious with pro-democracy bishops and wanted the pope to keep them in line. Throughout the trip, the pope defended human rights. Many believe that the seeds of the "people power" revolution that

The cross and the spear. With Fijian warriors, Suva, Fiji,
November 21, 1986. Luciano Mellace/Reuters

Among the faithful. At Rome's World Youth Day, August 19, 2000. Paolo Cocco/Reuters

would sweep the country in 1985 and 1986 were sown during the pope's visit. Galvanized in part by what the pope had said in 1981, Cardinal Jaime Sin, the ever-smiling but steely willed cardinal archbishop of Manila, and other pro-democracy bishops stepped up their criticism of the repressive Marcos regime. In 1983 opposition leader Benigno "Ninoy" Aquino was killed at Manila airport as he returned from exile. The opposition grew stronger and was unified when his widow, Corazon Aquino, announced her candidacy for president in a snap election Marcos had called for February 1986. Cardinal Sin and his bishops backed the National Citizens Movement for Free Elections. The elections were rigged and Marcos won. Sin and the bishops pressed on despite some nervousness in the Vatican about their political involvement. The bishops, broadcasting on the Church's Radio Veritas, called for nonviolent demonstrations and passive resistance. Two generals broke with Marcos and declared that Aquino was the legitimate president. Only the human shield of hundreds of thousands of people

A heavenly hosing down. A fireman in Rome cools a
sweltering crowd in St. Peter's Square for World Youth Day,
August 15, 2000. Paul Hanna/Reuters

organized and directed by the Church protected the rebel
generals from Marcos loyalists, preventing a bloodbath
and possibly a civil war. Ferdinand and Imelda Marcos left
for exile in Hawaii, and Sin flew to Rome to be
congratulated by a relieved pope.

Papal visits to several other countries also helped galvanize
people to stand up to dictators. When he made a lightning
visit to Port-au-Prince, Haiti, in 1983, the pope lectured
President Jean-Claude "Baby Doc" Duvalier, whose corrupt

family had kept the people of what was then the Western
Hemisphere's poorest country in misery while enriching
themselves. After the visit, grassroots religious
movements, using audiotapes of the pope's anti-Duvalier
homily, took up his call for change. In 1986, "Baby Doc"
and his elegant wife fled to exile in France. One of the
leaders of that revolution, Father Jean-Bertrand Aristide,
became president in 1991, but by that time he had been
expelled from his religious order for his advocacy of
violent class struggle to achieve social justice.

The pope blesses the bones of two Mexican martyrs at a beatification mass, Mexico City, August 1, 2002. Andrew Winning/Reuters

When the pope visited Paraguay in 1988, General Alfredo Stroessner was in his 35th year of uninterrupted power. A few days before the start of the visit, Stroessner banned a scheduled meeting between the pope and the opposition umbrella group Constructors of Society. It was an unprecedented standoff. The Vatican refused to blink, and Stroessner backed down for the first time in more than three decades. "Even dictators know when to give in," recalled Cardinal Tucci. The meeting took place in a sports arena where political opponents, many of them university students, put tape over their mouths to show that they had no voice in society. It was an unheard-of challenge to the iron rule of Stroessner and his Colorado Party. Less than a year later, Stroessner was overthrown in a coup and fled to Brazil. Free elections followed, and Paraguay too entered the club of Latin American democracies.

In 1987 the pope visited Chile while General Augusto Pinochet still held a vice-like grip on the country. There too the visit gave opponents a chance to air their views before the world media. Students took to the streets of Santiago chanting "Juan Pablo, Hermano, Quitanos El Tirano" (John Paul, brother, take away the tyrant). In planning for the trip, the Vatican organizers insisted that the pope meet with the political opposition. The pope had set the tone even before he arrived by telling reporters aboard his plane that Pinochet "will fall sooner or later." The year after the visit, a national plebiscite rejected military rule. Pinochet's slow but steady fall from power had begun.

Homegrown Halos, 20th Century Crucifixions

Pope John Paul made more saints and "blesseds" (the last step before sainthood) than all his predecessors combined. From the start of his papacy he felt it was important to reflect the Church's universal nature by holding ceremonies to create saints or blesseds on the soil where they had lived. So he went all the way to Madagascar, Papua New Guinea, Australia and South Korea to honor local religious luminaries. He continued the practice even when frailty began to take its toll. In the summer of 2002, when he was 82, he added Guatemala and Mexico to an already long trip to Canada in order to hold three canonization and beatification ceremonies.

His visits often brought comfort to local churches that had suffered. In 1982, on one of his first trips to Africa, the pope insisted that aides add to his itinerary a stop in Equatorial Guinea. The tiny West African nation had a population of some 350,000—less than some Rome neighborhoods—but a tragic recent past. In 1972 Francisco Macias Nguema named himself president for life and began a reign of terror that virtually sealed off the country from the outside world. Arrests and summary executions were the order of the day. Priests who dared to oppose him were crucified, their bodies left hanging under the African sun as a warning to others. Macias was overthrown in 1979 and later executed. The pope told reporters on the plane taking him to that African trip, "When my aides told me what had happened there, I told them 'We have to go. We have to go. Find a way to go.'"

Once, though, the pope did not get his way. During the war in Bosnia in 1994, the curia convinced him to scrap plans to visit the capital Sarajevo as a "pilgrim of peace" after besieging Bosnian Serb forces refused to guarantee the safety of the local population. The visit went ahead in 1997, after the war had ended.

In 1993, the pope made his first trip to countries of the former Soviet Union, a seven-day pilgrimage that would have been unthinkable just four years earlier. Lithuania, the most Catholic of the Baltic Republics, had paid a huge price during communism, with hundreds of thousands of people, including bishops and priests, shipped off to die in Siberian work camps during the Stalinist era. The pope paid tribute to Catholics who had suffered from communist oppression when he visited the Hill of Crosses near the northern town of Siauliai. The hill had become a symbol of freedom, first against imperialist Russia in the 19th century and later against Soviet totalitarianism. Catholics had planted thousands of wooden crosses there as a sign of their faith and yearning for freedom. In the 19th century the Tsar's soldiers would burn the crosses down. In the 20th century communist bulldozers razed them. But they were always re-erected. When the pope visited in 1993, he walked through a forest of more than 10,000 crosses, some only inches high, others so tall it looked as if he were walking through a field of corn, ramrod straight on a windless day.

In Albania in 1993 the pope paid tribute to the priests who had been left to die at the bottom of mine shafts in what

Stalinist dictator Enver Hoxha had proudly proclaimed the world's first officially atheist state. In the northern city of Shkoder, he consecrated four new bishops, including one who had been condemned to death on trumped up charges of being a Vatican spy. The same year he added a nine-hour stop in Sudan to an already planned trip to Africa. In a tense meeting in Khartoum, he stared down the country's radical Islamist leaders and demanded that they respect the rights of Christians in the south.

Separating the (Communist) Men from the Boys

Two trips, 15 years apart, highlighted the risks and rewards of papal visits for hosts who happened to be convinced Marxists. Nicaragua in 1983 and Cuba in 1998 were studies in communist contrast. Both revolved around two commandantes, Daniel Ortega and Fidel Castro. Ortega is probably still regretting his decision to allow the pope to stop in the Central American country. Castro, all things considered, is probably content. Nicaragua, then run by the Sandinistas, was home to a so-called Popular Church the government hoped could eventually replace the institutional Church. The Iglesia Popular was made up of small communist-style "base communities" which often identified Christian liberation with violent revolution. Nicaragua was a media packaging dream come true—all of the region's political, religious and social problems conveniently squeezed into a tiny country that was to be the main focus of a papal tour of Central America in March 1983. Nicaragua's archbishop, Miguel Obando y Bravo, had supported the 1979 Sandinista revolution against the corrupt, U.S.-backed Somoza family dictatorship. But later he fell out with the Sandinistas over civil rights and democratic reforms. To counter the bishop's influence, the Sandinistas recruited two priests, Miguel D'Escoto and Ernesto Cardenal, to the revolutionary government where they served in open defiance of the Vatican. The Alitalia jet carrying the pope finally landed in Managua on March 4. Ortega, dressed in military fatigues, delivered a vitriolic anti-American diatribe under the hot sun. One of the office-holding priests, Culture Minister Ernesto Cardenal, stood in the receiving line on the airport tarmac wearing a white collarless shirt and a white beret. In a scene that became famous around the world, Cardenal knelt and the pope wagged his finger above his head and told him in Spanish: "You must straighten out your position in the Church."

The arrival ceremony was just an appetizer for a spectacular confrontation that was to come. The Sandinistas had installed a second, secret sound system at the venue for an open-air mass where the pope concluded his one-day visit. They also packed the front section of the field with their supporters. When the pope read parts of his homily that were unfavorable to the regime, the Sandinistas lowered the volume of his microphone and raised the volume of those that had been planted among government supporters. The Sandinista agitators shouted down the pope with slogans such as "Poder Popular" (people power). Clearly irritated, the pope had to shout "Silencio!" (Silence!). To make matters worse, the Sandinistas violated an agreement with the Vatican to remove huge billboards displaying Marxist revolutionary heroes from the altar stage. It was impossible to dismantle them at the last minute.

The Sandinistas' attempt to get the pope to bless their revolution backfired miserably. Recalling that day nearly 20 years later, Cardinal Tucci, then a simple priest, said the Sandinistas had been doubly stupid. "First, they treated the pope the way they did. Second, they allowed the whole world to see it happening," Tucci said. National television stations from each of the Central American nations had agreed to broadcast every event live to all of the countries. "Everybody saw the sacrilege that was happening as it happened, the entire region saw that a papal mass was being desecrated and that the Sandinistas had tried to hijack it for political reasons," Tucci said. When the papal party returned to their base in San Jose, Costa Rica, late that night, they were stunned to see hundreds of thousands of people on the streets. Television and radio stations in Costa Rica had urged people to pour out of their homes to take part in an "act of reparation" for the "sacrilegious events" in Managua and to "console the pope."

Calling a priest into line. The pope wags his finger at Father Ernesto Cardenal, who held office in Nicaragua's revolutionary government in defiance of papal orders to step down, Managua, March 4, 1983. Mario Tapia/Reuters

God's Man in Havana

By contrast, the pope's long-awaited visit to Cuba in January 1998 went off mostly without a hitch. Another "commandante," a grayer, older and wiser Fidel Castro, decided after lengthy negotiations with the Vatican that he would go with the flow. "Castro told me that the pope could go where he wanted and say what he wanted. Whether he (Castro) would agree with what was being said was another matter," Cardinal Tucci recalled. "Castro handled it very well."

While Castro's government had repressed the Catholic Church after the 1959 revolution, the restrictions were never on the scale of those of the communist regimes in Eastern Europe. But the government did keep firm control, denying the Church access to the media and severely limiting visas for foreign priests and nuns. In the months leading up to the visit, Castro and his government slowly gave in to Vatican requests. Joaquin Navarro-Valls, the papal spokesman, coaxed some of the most significant concessions out of Castro. Navarro-Valls, a suave Spaniard with a strong presence who exuded an air of total self-confidence, spoke one-on-one with Castro for seven hours in one of the Cuban leader's famous and rambling nocturnal meetings. Over food, Spanish wine and a concluding cigar, Navarro-Valls succeeded where Vatican diplomats had failed. He convinced Castro that Cuba's international image could gain much if the trip were highly successful and if prepared by certain gestures beforehand. Castro agreed to declare that Christmas 1997, a month before the pope's arrival, would be celebrated as a national feast for the first time since the revolution. Navarro-Valls also cajoled Castro into approving about 60 more visas for foreign priests and nuns. A number of other issues were sorted out to the Vatican's general satisfaction before the trip began.

On January 21, 1998, the pope landed in Havana. His hope for the entire visit was perhaps encapsulated in one short line of his arrival address: "May Cuba, with all its magnificent potential, open itself to the world and may the world open itself up to Cuba." With the aging commandante Castro standing beside him in a double-breasted suit instead of his military fatigues, the pope said Cubans deserved "freedom, mutual trust, social justice and lasting peace." For the first time in 40 years, Castro took a back seat. For five days in January, he stood in the shadows while Cubans shouted hosannas to someone else and chanted "Libertad, Libertad, Libertad" (Freedom, Freedom, Freedom). Despite the unprecedented protests, the pope gave Castro something to glow about. On several occasions, the pontiff blasted the United States' economic embargo against the island.

When he returned to Rome, the pope said he hoped that his visit to Cuba would bear "fruit" similar to that which his first trip to Poland had brought to his homeland. When the pope was elected in 1978, Soviet leader Leonid Brezhnev told Poland's communist leaders that they would be insane ever to allow the pope to visit Poland. They said they had little choice. He was, after all, a Polish citizen. Brezhnev reportedly told them they could bar him because he was no longer a Polish citizen. When Castro waved goodbye to the pope at Havana's airport on the warm tropical evening of January 25, 1998, he knew he had taken a gamble, just as Polish leaders had taken a gamble nearly two decades earlier when they let the pope make his first trip to Poland. And Brezhnev, whose predecessor Josef Stalin once asked mockingly "How many divisions does the pope have?" was right. The pope was no longer a Polish citizen but a citizen of the world.

In His Own Words

"He was never a Christian and he never pretended to be a Christian, but I learned a lot from him. Christians could learn from him about how to be Christians. I learned a lot from him and I am not ashamed to say this," speaking of Mahatma Gandhi after praying at his memorial during a visit to India in 1986.

"You have to know that 'prison' to appreciate this freedom," to reporters who tracked him down in the northern Italian mountains in 1987, the first summer he took a holiday away from the papal summer residence south of Rome.

"It has never been easy to accept the Gospel teaching in its entirety, and it never will be," addressing American Catholics during a trip to the United States in 1987.

"But other people climb to the top, don't they?" overruling aides who had advised him not to try to climb to the top of a mountain in northern Italy in 1987.

"Why be afraid of showing yourself to be a man among men?" to reporters during a 1988 holiday after being photographed in hiking clothes.

"Behold the night is over, day has dawned anew," speaking to Czechs and Slovaks in 1990 during his first trip to a country of the former communist East Bloc outside his native Poland after the fall of the Berlin Wall.

"God once said 'Do not kill.' No human group, Mafia or whatever, can trample on this most sacred law of God. In the name of the crucified and risen Christ…convert. One day the judgment of God will arrive," denouncing the Mafia during a trip to Sicily in 1993.

Unholy chaos at 33,000 feet. A group of reporters throngs
around the pope aboard a plane taking him on one of his
international trips in the early 1980s. Philip Pullella, associate
editor of the book and author of this chapter, is seen with the
moustache behind the pope. Luciano Mellace/Reuters

The Pope Meets Castro, Havana Airport, January 21, 1998

By Frances Kerry

Churches gleamed under new paint, choirs jubilantly rehearsed and some people had visions of a catalytic clash between the pope and Fidel Castro. It was as though the pontiff might fly into Havana, kiss the Cuban soil, square off against the man who had run the island for nearly four decades and cast a spark to ignite political change, as he had done nearly 20 years earlier in his homeland. But the Caribbean island of 11 million people, one of the world's last communist nations, turned out not to be a tinderbox, at least not at that time and not for that visitor.

President Castro, who was then 71, towered solicitously over the 77-year-old visitor when they met at Havana airport in January 1998. When the two were seen together in public during the trip, he slowed his gait and sometimes extended a protective hand toward the frail, white-robed figure—a respectful host who had told Cubans, believers and nonbelievers alike, to welcome the pope as a leading figure of the age, not a threat to the revolution.

The pope peppered his homilies with carefully worded criticism of the system, speaking at masses celebrated in squares accustomed to revolutionary rallies and now crowded with believers, Communist Party supporters and the curious. Nuns and neighbors rose daily to salute him when he woke in the Vatican envoy's residence in Havana, singing from a sidewalk where flowers were planted to welcome him and where street lights were on at night for the first time in years.

During those five breezy January days, you could tune into state media and hear the Communist Party's world view replaced, astonishingly, with religious music and prayer as the papal masses were broadcast live. But in a country that had never been as fervently Roman Catholic as many of its Latin American neighbors and where a generation had grown up with the Church sidelined, the papal presence was more of an exotic spectacle than a spiritual homecoming for many Cubans. It was only in 1992 that Cuba had turned from being officially an atheist state to a secular one.

The visit opened an extraordinary window to words of political dissent, in public and on state television, and not just from the pope. The Archbishop of Santiago, Pedro Meurice, icily criticized the one-party monolith during the papal mass in that city. There were cries of "Freedom!" from the crowd at the pope's last mass, in Havana's vast Revolution Square, the Church's place for a day with a painting of Jesus Christ looming over the altar and the Jesuit-educated Castro listening meekly among the congregation.

The Church, long in the shadows, had bloomed as authorities dribbled out concessions before the visit—Christmas Day was made a holiday for the first time in decades, and Cardinal Jaime Ortega, Archbishop of Havana, was allowed on state television to talk about the pope. The pontiff wanted the Church's flowering to continue and grow. Days after flying out of Havana, he said he also hoped his trip might inspire opponents of communism in the way his first papal journey home to Poland had done in 1979.

But although the Cuban leader, in power since 1959, had had to endure public criticism, the visit had been orderly. Castro was also buoyed by the pope's condemnation of the longstanding U.S. economic embargo against the island—a blow to Washington's policy of isolation.

As the pope's visit ended, Castro mocked those who had expected, or hoped, it might deliver an "apocalyptic" punch to the political system in Cuba. It was not apocalyptic, but in some ways the island would never be the same.

As time goes by. Fidel Castro and the pope consult the Cuban president's watch as the pope arrives in Havana for a historic visit, January 21, 1998. Zoraida Diaz/Reuters

A day with the circus. The pope watches an acrobat leaving after kissing his hand following a performance of circus artists in the Vatican, January 23, 1985. Luciano Mellace/Reuters

The pope's helicopter blows the cassocks of Polish bishops as
it lands, Elblag, Poland, June 6, 1999. Jerry Lampen/Reuters

The orator. Giving a speech to young people at the Santiago National Stadium in Chile, April 3, 1987. Oscar Sabetta/Reuters

With Chilean General Augusto Pinochet during a difficult visit to Chile, April 1, 1987. Nancy McGirr/Reuters

A young Hutu refugee hides behind his mother's dress with a papal design during a visit by the pope to Gikongoro, Rwanda, July 6, 1994. Jack Dabaghian/Reuters

With Princess Diana and Prince Charles at the Vatican, April 25, 1985. Vatican photo

U.S. President Bill Clinton applauds the pope, St. Louis, January 26, 1999. Gary Hershorn/Reuters

The pope with Indian Prime Minister Rajiv Gandhi and his
Italian-born wife Sonia in New Delhi, February 1, 1986.
Luciano Mellace/Reuters

Two African girls in native garb greet the pope in Togo, August 9, 1985. Luciano Mellace/Reuters

African wind. A gust of wind blows the pope's cape over his
head as a woman hands him flowers in the Ivory Coast, 1990.
Luciano Mellace/Reuters

Titans of the Century

By Paul Holmes

There are few occasions in a career as a journalist when you sense you are in the presence of greatness. I had one such experience in South Africa in September 1995 when two of the towering figures of the 20th century, both already in their mid-70s, came together.

Pope John Paul, the churchman who helped hasten the demise of communism in Eastern Europe, and President Nelson Mandela, the symbol of the struggle against apartheid, met in Pretoria at the building that had served for decades as the residence of white minority presidents.

The pope was on his first official trip to South Africa, a country he had previously shunned because of its racist policies. After all-race elections that ended three centuries of white rule and elevated Mandela to the highest office in the land, he had come to honor a man whose long years in jail had made him, in the pope's own words, "a silent, suffering witness of your people's yearning for true liberation."

I had been designated as a Vatican "pool reporter" for the meeting. At events where access is limited, these reporters share their material with everyone else in the press party. Papal meetings with presidents are often courtesy calls, so being a pool reporter can be equivalent to drawing the short straw. Photographers and camera crews are ushered into the meeting room for a quick "grip and grin" shot and then hustled out. Text reporters loiter outside and are lucky to get a briefing from the official Vatican or presidential spokesman.

Profiles in courage. The pope and Nelson Mandela, who both survived oppressive regimes, South Africa, September 16, 1995. Luciano Mellace/Reuters

This time was different. First there was a handshake and a brief conversation with Mandela as he entered the state house to await the pope. Then, after the private talks were over, we reporters were invited into the official reception to mingle with the 180 guests—politicians, diplomats, clerics and, perhaps incongruously, the British actress Liz Hurley, who had been filming in South Africa.

The affair was typical of the informality that Mandela brought to his job. I stood a yard or so from the pope as Mandela presented the dignitaries in the receiving line. It was impossible not to hear what was said and, for me, hard to resist a rush of excitement about the turn of events in South Africa when Mandela introduced the pope to another veteran of the anti-apartheid struggle, Mac Maharaj.

"This is the minister of transport," Mandela told the pope. "We were together in prison. He served 18 years."

Hunting souls, hunting heads. The pope watches a tribe of
former headhunters dance in Shillong, India, February 4,
1986. Luciano Mellace/Reuters

Indira Gandhi stadium, New Delhi, February 2, 1986.
Luciano Mellace/Reuters

With Brazilian Indians, Cuiaba, Brazil, October 16, 1991.
Luciano Mellace/Reuters

A Cuban man holds up a poster of the pope, Camaguay, Cuba,
January 23, 1998. Gary Hershorn/Reuters

Animal lover. The pope pets Melinda, a young kangaroo, in
Adelaide, Australia, November 30, 1986. Will Burgess/Reuters

A popemobile without a crowd. Traveling through rural
Newfoundland, Canada, September 12, 1984.
Reuters/Andy Clark/courtesy of CP

An enthusiastic member of the crowd tugs on the pope's cassock in Canada, September 10, 1984. Reuters/Andy Clark/courtesy of CP

Chief to chief. Talking to an Algonquin Indian leader during a
tour of Canada, September 10, 1984. Reuters/Andy
Clark/courtesy of CP

Wearing the hard hat. The pope descends in an elevator on a visit to the Sulcis mines in Sardinia, Italy, 1985.
Luciano Mellace/Reuters

In the shadow of the Eiffel Tower, August 21, 1997.
Eric Galliard/Reuters

A papal train. A freak snow storm in Rome forced the papal plane to land in Naples in the middle of the night on his return from India. When the local cardinal was woken up and told he must find a train to take the pope to Rome, he thought it was a bad joke, February 11, 1986.

Luciano Mellace/Reuters

In a gondola on Venice's Grand Canal, June 16, 1985.
Luciano Mellace/Reuters

Bulgarian children peek from their kindergarten window
during a papal visit, Rakovski, Bulgaria, May 22, 2002.
Dimitar Dilkoff/Reuters

Armenian women at a papal mass in Etchmiadzin, Armenia,
September 27, 2001. Paolo Cocco/Reuters

Kazakh police with a poster of Pope John Paul in the
background in Astana, September 22, 2001.
Alexander Demianchuk/Reuters

A Greek Orthodox priest in a crowd with banners making their views known about a papal visit to Athens, Greece, May 2, 2001. Yiorgos Karahalis/Reuters

Hindu children protest against the pope's visit, New Delhi, January 31, 1986. Arthur Tsang/Reuters

Greeting Muslim clerics, Cairo, Egypt, February 24, 2000.
Mona Sharaf/Reuters

Strapped in. The pope in a helicopter bound for Bethlehem, March 22, 2000. Israeli Government Press Office

With Palestinian leader Yasser Arafat at the Dehaishe refugee camp, March 22, 2000. Havakuk Levison/Reuters

The lamb and the lions. Israeli security forces protect the
pope in Jerusalem, March 23, 2000. Mal Langsdon/Reuters

An olive branch in the Holy Land. Young Palestinian novice
nuns throw olive branches before the pope, Korazim, Israel,
March 24, 2000. Mal Langsdon/Reuters

A wing and a prayer. Arriving in Kazakhstan, September 22, 2001. Paolo Cocco/Reuters

Children of the Same God: Pope John Paul and the Jewish People

Alan Elsner

Pope John Paul slowly, haltingly made his way to the Western Wall, the last remaining remnant of Jerusalem's Second Jewish Temple, destroyed by the Romans in the year 70 A.D. A few feet from the Wall, the cardinals accompanying him stepped away, leaving the pope to proceed shakily alone. He bowed his head in silent prayer, touched the ancient stones, placed a note in a crack between the giant slabs and blessed the note. It read: "God of our fathers, You chose Abraham and his descendants to bring Your Name to the nations. We are deeply saddened by the behavior of those who in the course of history have caused these children of yours to suffer, and asking forgiveness, we wish to commit ourselves to genuine brotherhood with the people of the covenant."

The pope's visit on March 26, 2000, to the holiest site in Judaism and his plea for forgiveness was immediately and almost universally hailed as one of the most dramatic and important moments of his long pontificate. Many Israelis and Jews around the world were intensely moved. But the pontiff's dramatic and symbolic act perhaps carried an even more important message for Catholics.

For almost 2,000 years, the Church had insisted that the Temple had been destroyed as a sign that God had withdrawn His favor from the Jewish people as a punishment for their refusal to accept Jesus as the Messiah.

Throughout the centuries, the Church taught its adherents to feel contempt and hatred for Jews and Judaism and was complicit in persecution. Popes and saints alike preached that the Jews were a cursed people, dispersed around the world, condemned to misery as witnesses to the truth of the Christian faith. Some historians say this teaching eventually helped lay the groundwork for the Shoah, or Holocaust—the murder of six million Jews by the Nazis during World War Two.

So entrenched were these ideas that Catholics in their Easter liturgy continued to refer to the "perfidious Jews" until the 1960s.

By stepping reverentially to the Western Wall, the pope was symbolically repudiating such teachings. He was demonstrating that in his eyes, the spirit of God had not departed from the site of the Temple, and therefore that God's covenant with the Jewish people had never been revoked. Rabbi Michael Melchior, the Israeli cabinet minister who greeted the pope at the Wall, said after the visit, "It has theological significance—the recognition of the end of the period of humiliation of the Jewish nation. It is recognition of our right to return to our land and this place."

Father John Pawlikowski, director of Catholic–Jewish Studies at the Catholic Theological Union at the University of Chicago, reflecting the views of many Catholics, called it one of the strongest moments in John Paul's pontificate, the climax of more than two decades of steady effort to confront and try to make amends for the "dark side of Catholic history."

Even papal critics, like author and former priest James Carroll, who has argued that John Paul has been a disaster for the Catholic Church, were impressed and moved. "The current pope has done more to heal the breach between Christians and Jews, and in particular between Catholics and Jews, than any previous pope. The culmination of John Paul's work was his historic act of repentance in 2000, coupled with his visit to Jerusalem and his pilgrimage to the Western Wall. This act symbolically reversed 2,000 years of Christian denigration of the Temple and of the rights of Jews to be at home in Jerusalem and Israel. With that simple nonverbal act, the pope made a major move away from one of the most powerful and poisonous aspects of Christian theology. It is one of the most important things his pontificate has accomplished," Carroll said.

Still, for Carroll and other papal critics, both Jewish and Catholic, the pope's dramatic actions and utterances on the Jews and Judaism remained partial achievements. They feel he should have gone further. "The real horror of Christian anti-Semitism, so public and so constant, has yet to be fully confronted," Carroll said.

Pope John Paul's long journey to the Wall began in his hometown of Wadowice in Poland. Much has been written about how the young Karol Wojtyla grew up side by side with Jews, who at that time formed at least 20 percent of the population. Wojtyla had Jewish friends, including Jerzy Kluger, who moved to Rome after the war and rekindled his friendship with Wojtyla after he became pope.

The young Wojtyla even occasionally played goalie on a Jewish soccer team. In 1937 he and his father attended a performance by the famed Jewish cantor Moishe Kussawieki in the Wadowice synagogue.

During the years leading to the outbreak of World War Two, anti-Semitism was rampant in Poland, driven both by right-wing nationalists and the traditional anti-Judaism of the Church. On February 29, 1936, the Primate of Poland, Cardinal Augustus Hlond, issued a letter in which he urged Poles to boycott Jewish businesses and attacked Jews as Bolshevik free-thinkers, atheists, usurers and peddlers of pornography and prostitution. "As long as Jews exist, a Jewish problem exists and will continue to exist," the cardinal declared.

But Wojtyla, inspired by the strong moral example of his father, was never drawn into anti-Semitism. A childhood friend, Ginka Beer, later said, "There was only one family who never showed any racial hostility towards us, and that was Lolek and his dad."

Kluger recounted how he once rushed excitedly into a church to tell his friend Karol that they would be classmates the following year. He found his friend assisting in a service and sat down to wait until it was finished. A woman, knowing that Kluger was Jewish, asked what he was doing there. After the service, Wojtyla asked Kluger, "By the way, what was that old woman saying to you?" Kluger said, "She asked me if I was the son of the president of the Jewish community. I don't think she thought I belonged here. Maybe she was surprised to see a Jew in church."

To which the future pope said: "Why? Aren't we all God's children?"

When Wojtyla was elected pope, the initial reaction from world Jewry was far from positive. "There was enormous skepticism. The feeling was, he's a Pole so he's got to be an anti-Semite. The opposite turned out to be true, precisely because of his background, his experience of the Shoah, what he saw with his own eyes. He was the right man for the right time. We will never see his like again," said Rabbi James Rudin, who for many years was in charge of Catholic–Jewish dialogue for the American–Jewish Committee. Rudin met Pope John Paul ten times over the years of his pontificate and accompanied him on the pilgrimage to Israel in 2000. But he particularly recalled one meeting that took place at the Vatican in March 1990.

"I was leading an American–Jewish delegation. After the formal speeches, we stayed to chat, and one of us mentioned we were going on to Poland the next day. The pope immediately became very animated and almost rhapsodic. He said, 'Wadowice, Friday afternoon, candles, psalms, people walking to synagogue.' It was totally genuine. In that moment, in his mind he was back in Wadowice, remembering with affection the Jews walking to synagogue to welcome the Sabbath. He was a living witness to a scene that can never take place again because that community was destroyed in the Shoah and most of those people were murdered," Rudin said.

Pope John Paul expressed these same sentiments in his 1994 book *Crossing the Threshold of Hope*. He wrote: "I would like to return to the synagogue at Wadowice. It was destroyed by the Germans and no longer exists today. A few years ago, Jerzy [Kluger] came to me to say that the place where the synagogue had stood should be honored with a special commemorative plaque. I must admit that in that moment, we both felt a deep emotion. We saw faces of people we knew and cared for, and we recalled those Saturdays of our childhood and adolescence when the Jewish community of Wadowice gathered for prayer."

Though his childhood experiences of Jews remained with him, it was his direct experience of the Shoah that burned a searing memory that was to become a central part of Karol Wojtyla's spiritual identity. There is no evidence that Wojtyla, who spent the war in Krakow, played any part in organized efforts to help or shield Jews from the Nazis, although he may have helped individual Jews. During his visit to Israel, Edith Schiere, an Auschwitz survivor, told of meeting Wojtyla as she was staggering down the road after somehow escaping from the camp. She said he carried her to the train station on his back and brought her something to eat. The pope did not recall the incident. But he saw what was happening to his friends and neighbors. On March 13, 1943, Germans shot scores of Jews in Krakow's Zgoda Square, including Rabbi Seltenreich, the Klugers' rabbi from Wadowice.

In his book Pope John Paul wrote, "Then came the Second World War, with its concentration camps and systematic extermination. First and foremost, the sons and daughters of the Jewish nation were condemned for no other reason than that they were Jewish. Even if indirectly, whoever lived in Poland at that time came into contact with this reality. Therefore this was also a personal experience of mine, an experience I carry with me even today. Auschwitz, perhaps the most meaningful symbol of the

Holocaust of the Jewish people, shows to what lengths a system constructed on principles of racial hatred and greed for power can go."

On his first visit to Poland after becoming pope, in June 1979, John Paul visited Auschwitz, where he declared, "The Shoah has continued to cast a shadow. This terrible tragedy has challenged both Jews and Christians. It has made us reflect not only on those short but horribly evil years of Nazi rule in Germany but on the almost 2,000 years of Jewish–Christian relations."

For many, it seems astonishing to think that when the pope made a historic visit to the Great Synagogue in Rome on April 13, 1986—a five-minute car ride across the River Tiber from the Vatican—it was the first time that any pope had ever set foot in a synagogue. It becomes less surprising after examining traditional Catholic teachings. For

With Italian rabbis in Rome during the first ever visit by a pope to a synagogue, April 13, 1986. Luciano Mellace/Reuters

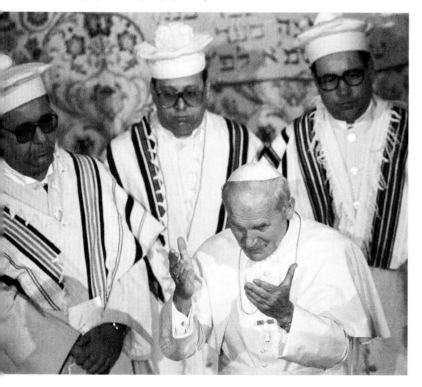

example, Saint John Chrysostom, a fourth-century patriarch of Constantinople, called the synagogue "a brothel...a den of robbers and a lodging for wild beasts" and openly called for Jews to be killed. "Although such beasts are unfit for work, they are fit for killing," he said.

Saint Augustine (354–430) helped formulate the teaching that guided the Church in its attitude to the Jews up to the 1960s. "Jews are not to be killed," he wrote. "They have killed Christ but Christ, speaking through David, urges the Church to protect the Jews, who nonetheless are the enemy bearing the mark of Cain."

Over the centuries of humiliations punctuated by massacres and expulsions, some popes did try to protect Jews, although none challenged the idea that they were a cursed and guilty people. Innocent IV (who was pope from 1243–54) condemned the blood libel widely circulated throughout Christendom that held that Jews murdered Christian children and used their blood to bake Passover matzas, or unleavened bread. Benedict XII (1334–42) tried, without great success, to protect the Jews of Germany from a wave of massacres following accusations that they desecrated the Host. Clement VI (1342–52) issued an edict in 1348 against the myth that Jews were responsible for the Black Death.

But others took a harsher view. Innocent III (1198–1216) required Jews to wear distinctive clothing, such as the "Jewish hat" or "Jewish badge," a technique later copied by the Nazis. Gregory IX (1227–41) prompted the burnings of sacred Jewish texts that continued off and on for centuries.

Long after other parts of Europe had torn down the walls of their Jewish ghettoes, successive popes kept Jews in the cities under their control locked up in overcrowded, disease-ridden quarters. Pius IX (1846–78), who was beatified by John Paul in 2000, presided over Europe's last ghetto in Rome itself until 1870. This same pope was accused of complicity in the kidnapping and forced baptism of a Jewish child, Edgardo Mortara.

Cardinal Edward Cassidy, who headed the Vatican Commission for Religious Relations with the Jews in the 1990s, summed up the Church's record: "There can be no denial of the fact that from the time of the Emperor Constantine on, Jews were isolated and discriminated against in the Christian world. There were expulsions and forced conversions. Literature propagated stereotypes,

Auschwitz survivors with the pope at the Nazi extermination camp, 1979. Jan Morek/FORUM

Poles gathered to see the pope during his visit to Auschwitz look through barbed wire once used to keep death camp inmates from escaping. Aleksander Jalosinski/FORUM

preaching accused Jews of every age of deicide; the ghetto, which came into being in 1555 with a papal bull, became in Nazi Germany the antechamber of the extermination."

Some historians would go further, directly implicating the Church in the modern, racial doctrine of anti-Semitism. "As modern anti-Semitic movements took shape at the end of the 19th century, the Church was a major player in them, constantly warning people of the rising 'Jewish peril,'" wrote David I. Kertzer in a study of the actions and attitudes of 19th- and early 20th-century popes.

Pope John XXIII (1958–63) inspired the Vatican's first attempt to come to terms with this bitter legacy. In 1960 he held an important meeting with the French–Jewish historian Jules Isaac, who had published a groundbreaking study of Christian attitudes toward Judaism, which he characterized as a "teaching of contempt." Two years later, Pope John convened the Second Vatican Council, which eventually produced the milestone declaration "Nostra Aetate" (In Our Time). Finally, the Church felt ready to declare that the Jewish people could not be held collectively guilty for the death of Jesus. "The Jews should

Brotherhood in bloom. A man in Genzano, Italy, puts the finishing touches to a floral panel depicting the historic 1986 embrace between the pope and Rabbi Elio Toaff in the Rome synagogue, June 18, 2000. Alessia Pierdomenico/Reuters

not be presented as repudiated or cursed by God," the document said. "Jews remain very close to God…since God does not take back the gifts he bestowed or the choice he made."

Wojtyla, then a bishop little known outside of Poland, took part in the heated internal discussions that led up to that declaration, challenging Vatican conservatives who still saw no need for change. But in 1968, when the Communist authorities in Poland launched a new and vicious anti-Semitic campaign that forced 34,000 Jews to hurriedly pack their bags and flee the country, Catholic leaders, Cardinal Wojtyla among them, remained silent.

It was only after his election as pope that Wojtyla began speaking publicly. In a series of forceful statements, the pope made it clear he was determined to put Catholic–Jewish relations on a totally new footing. Wherever he traveled around the world, he met with local Jewish leaders. As a key part of this outreach, he began preparing the ground for the Vatican to end its long refusal to recognize the state of Israel as the Jewish homeland. In a homily at Otranto in 1980, the pontiff recalled that the Jews, who had suffered "tragic experiences connected with the extermination of so many sons and daughters, were driven by a desire for security to set up the state of Israel." At the same time, he said, Palestinians had a right to a homeland.

At the conclusion of a visit to Brazil in 1991, the pope led a special prayer echoing Ezekiel 34:13: "May our Jewish brothers and sisters who have been led out among the peoples and gathered from foreign lands and brought back to their own country to the land of their ancestors be able to live there in peace and security on the 'mountains of Israel' guarded by the protection of God, their true shepherd."

Speaking during a visit to Australia, he declared, "The Catholic faith is rooted in the eternal truths of the Hebrew Scriptures and in the irrevocable covenant made with Abraham. We, too, gratefully hold these same truths of our Jewish heritage and look upon you as our brothers and sisters in the Lord."

In a U.S. television documentary, Feliks Tych, director of the Jewish Museum in Warsaw, commented, "In leaving Poland, Wojtyla freed himself to act, to start the re-education program regarding Jews in the Church, to forge diplomatic ties with Israel, to write the document on the Shoah."

If actions speak louder than words, Pope John Paul's actions spoke volumes. "Jews and Catholics all over the world have observed John Paul II meet with leaders of Jewish communities," said Rabbi Michael Signer, a theologian at Notre Dame University. "They witnessed his kneeling in prayer at Auschwitz. When he visited the synagogue in the city of Rome, people noticed that he did not sit on a platform raised above the Rabbi. He sat on the same platform with the Rabbi."

On that historic occasion in 1986 the pope delivered one of his strongest statements on Judaism: "The Jewish religion is not extrinsic to us, but in a certain way is intrinsic to our own religion. With Judaism, therefore, we have a relationship that we do not have with any other religion. You are our dearly beloved brothers and, in a certain way, it could be said that you are our elder brothers," he declared.

In 1994 the pope hosted a moving concert at the Vatican to honor the victims of the Shoah. Survivors joined the pontiff to listen as a setting of the Kaddish, the Jewish prayer for the dead, was played at the spiritual center of Christianity. Rabbi Rudin was there and recalled the pope swaying with emotion. "I think the pope had the faces of his dead classmates before his eyes," he said.

As a result of Pope John Paul's leadership, a major change in Catholic attitudes to Judaism began to permeate all ranks of the Church. Clergy and laity, especially in Europe and the United States, began to examine their consciences and make changes. "The textbooks used in Catholic schools have been radically overhauled and improved. You won't find any negative stereotypes of Jews and Judaism in our teaching materials any more. We don't actively try to convert Jews any more. We express respect for Jews and their religion," said Eugene Fisher, director of Catholic–Jewish relations at the U.S. Conference of Catholic Bishops.

In October 2000 some 150 Jewish theologians and rabbis issued a statement entitled "Dabru Emet" (Speaking the Truth), responding to the great progress that had been achieved. The statement recognized a dramatic change in Christianity in recent decades and offered eight precepts for future dialogue. These included the fact that Jews and

Poland during World War Two, 1939–1945

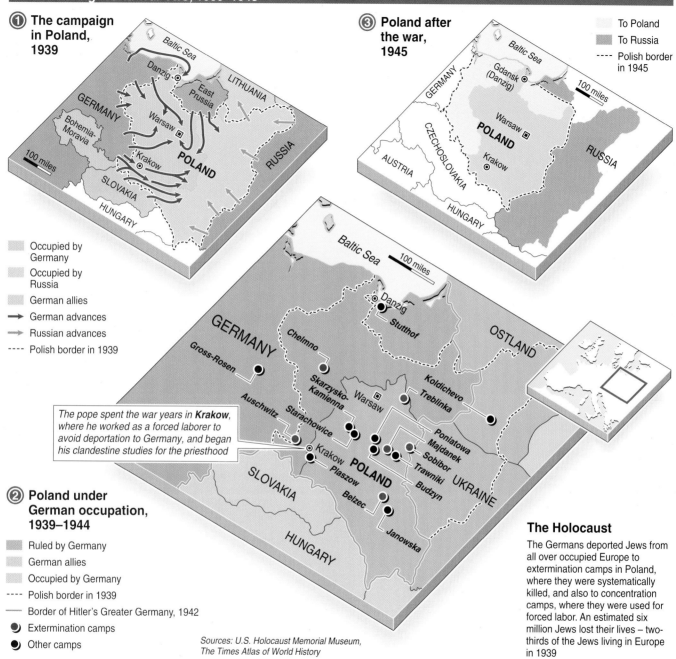

① **The campaign in Poland, 1939**

Baltic Sea
Danzig
East Prussia
LITHUANIA
GERMANY
Bohemia-Moravia
Warsaw
POLAND
Krakow
RUSSIA
SLOVAKIA
HUNGARY

100 miles

Occupied by Germany
Occupied by Russia
German allies
→ German advances
→ Russian advances
---- Polish border in 1939

② **Poland under German occupation, 1939–1944**

Ruled by Germany
German allies
Occupied by Germany
---- Polish border in 1939
— Border of Hitler's Greater Germany, 1942
◐ Extermination camps
◑ Other camps

*The pope spent the war years in **Krakow**, where he worked as a forced laborer to avoid deportation to Germany, and began his clandestine studies for the priesthood*

Baltic Sea
100 miles
Danzig
Stutthof
GERMANY
Chelmno
OSTLAND
Gross-Rosen
Skarzysko-Kamienna
Koldichevo
Warsaw
Treblinka
Auschwitz
Starachowice
Krakow
Plaszow
Belzec
Janowska
POLAND
Poniatowa
Majdanek
Sobibor
Trawniki
Budzyn
UKRAINE
SLOVAKIA
HUNGARY

Sources: U.S. Holocaust Memorial Museum, The Times Atlas of World History

③ **Poland after the war, 1945**

To Poland
To Russia
---- Polish border in 1945

Baltic Sea
Gdansk (Danzig)
GERMANY
Warsaw
POLAND
Krakow
CZECHOSLOVAKIA
AUSTRIA
HUNGARY
RUSSIA

100 miles

The Holocaust

The Germans deported Jews from all over occupied Europe to extermination camps in Poland, where they were systematically killed, and also to concentration camps, where they were used for forced labor. An estimated six million Jews lost their lives – two-thirds of the Jews living in Europe in 1939

Christians worshipped the same God, that their two religions were based on common moral principles and that they could and should work together for peace and justice. It recognized that there would always be a divide between the two religions over whether or not Jesus was the Messiah, but said that this "humanly irreconcilable difference will not be settled until God redeems the entire world as promised in Scripture."

However, one statement—"Nazism was not a Christian phenomenon"—provoked considerable debate within the Jewish world, prompting some prominent Jewish figures to refuse to sign the statement. Rabbi Rudin was one. "I think it let the Church off the hook much too easily," he said.

There were other political stumbles in the relationship. Jews were angered when the pope formally received Kurt Waldheim at the Vatican in 1987. Other foreign governments had shunned the newly elected president of Austria, who had been placed on the U.S. Department of Justice's Watch List as a suspected war criminal. Waldheim had covered up his service as a Nazi Party member and German military intelligence officer in the Balkans during World War Two.

The pope's decision to receive Palestine Liberation Organization chief Yasser Arafat at the Vatican in September 1982 also raised hackles. The pope met Arafat and Israeli leaders regularly when they came to Rome and on each occasion repeated his call for Israel to have the right to live in security and for Palestinians to have a homeland. He also repeatedly called on both sides to renounce violence. In February 2000, on the eve of the pope's pilgrimage to the Holy Land, the Vatican and the PLO signed a basic agreement that warned Israel that any unilateral decisions affecting Jerusalem were "morally and legally unacceptable." The Vatican wants Jerusalem, which Israel has declared its "united and eternal" capital, to have international guarantees protecting it as a city sacred to Jews, Muslims and Christians.

Jews were also concerned when the Vatican issued a document entitled "Dominus Iesus" in 2000, stating that non-Catholic religions were "gravely deficient" and adding that interreligious dialogue was considered "part of the evangelizing mission of the Church." They were somewhat mollified by statements from senior cardinals that these words did not apply to Judaism. Some senior Church figures insisted that Catholics should not give up their attempts to convert Jews. Cardinal Avery Dulles, a theologian at Fordham University, argued that Christians had a duty to proclaim the truth of their religion to everyone, including Jews. "Once we grant that there are some persons for whom it is not important to acknowledge Christ, to be baptized and to receive the sacraments, we raise questions about our own religious life," he wrote.

However, by far the biggest irritant in Jewish–Catholic relations remained the dispute over painful history dividing the two religions and particularly the meaning of the Shoah.

One of the thorniest figures in Catholic–Jewish relations was Edith Stein, a convert from Judaism who became a Carmelite nun but was murdered at Auschwitz by the Nazis because she had been born as a Jew. In 1998, John Paul was to canonize Stein as Saint Teresa Benedicta of the Cross, an act that many Jews found hurtful, since it seemed to suggest that the only Jewish victim of the Shoah worthy of being venerated was a convert.

Others, including some prominent Catholics, suggested that the real reason for Stein's canonization was that she was a useful symbol who allowed the Church to contend that Catholics were targets and victims of Nazism rather than perpetrators. "The canonization of Edith Stein revealed the lengths to which the Church was prepared to go to renegotiate its own history during the Holocaust," said James Carroll.

Stein's niece, Suzanne Batzdorff, commented, "For Jews, I believe Edith Stein is a gulf, not a bridge. A convert from Judaism cannot be a role model for Jews. I've talked to many Catholics in the forefront of Jewish–Catholic dialogue who say they need a symbol for the Holocaust. Jews don't need a symbol because for us it's all too real; besides, almost every family has its own victim or victims."

In 1984 a group of Carmelite nuns devoted to Stein's memory moved into a building near the gates of

Canonization ceremony for Edith Stein, a nun who converted to Christianity from the Jewish faith and died in Auschwitz during World War Two, October 11, 1998. Paul Hanna/Reuters

Auschwitz where they committed themselves to offering Christian prayers. Jews around the world were outraged by their presence at a place where at least 1.1 million people were murdered, 90 percent of them Jewish. Angry Jews immediately launched an international campaign against efforts to "Christianize the Shoah." Passions and tempers raged for years, and the convent became a running sore in Jewish–Catholic relations. Polish nationalists and Catholic zealots planted hundreds of crosses in what is the biggest Jewish cemetery in the world. Eventually, John Paul intervened, asking the nuns to move to another building a short distance away. Most of the crosses were removed, but one giant, 20-foot high cross remained, the only religious symbol at the former extermination camp. It was the one originally erected for the pope during his 1979 mass.

When the pope visited Poland in 1999, Rabbi Menachem Joskowicz made a moving, unscripted appeal to him: "I would like to urge the pope to tell his people to take the last cross out of the camp so that Jews who come here can say their final prayer before dying." Underscoring the delicate nature of the cross dispute, Joskowicz was criticized by leaders of Warsaw's Jewish community for making the remarks.

In March 1998 the Vatican published "We Remember: A Reflection on the Shoah," which was supposed to be its definitive word on the meaning of the Holocaust. The Church expressed sorrow for the "failures of her sons and daughters in every age" and put forward the document as an act of teshuva, the Hebrew word for repentance. However, the document tried to draw a distinction between traditional anti-Jewish attitudes preached by the Church and Nazism, which it identified as a pagan ideology unconnected to Christianity. It went on to ask, "Did Christians give every possible assistance to those being persecuted, and in particular to the persecuted Jews? Many did but others did not." Many commentators seized on that sentence as a grotesque rewriting of history. Philip Cunningham, director of the Center for Christian–Jewish Learning at Boston College, called it a "singularly weak and ill-conceived formulation. In reality, some did [help Jews] and most did not." Catholic historian Gary Wills wrote, "Though expressions of sympathy for Jewish suffering are expressed in the new statement, it devotes more energy to exonerating the Church—and excoriating the Nazis for not following Church teachings—than to sympathizing with the Holocaust's victims."

Cardinal Edward Cassidy, head of the Vatican Commission for Religious Relations with Jews, which composed the Vatican's landmark document "We Remember" on the Holocaust, March 16, 1998. Max Rossi/Reuters

Rabbi Rudin saw "We Remember" as an attempt by the Vatican to distance itself from what critics say is at least indirect complicity in the Shoah. "If the narrative of the Shoah as set down in this document remains the definitive word of the Church, then we have a big problem," he said.

"We Remember" also included a defense of the wartime record of Pope Pius XII (1939–58), an intensely controversial and divisive figure, dubbed "Hitler's Pope" in John Cornwell's 1999 biography. Pius, a candidate for beatification, never once openly denounced the Nazi genocide against the Jews, although critics say he had abundant information that it was under way. The Vatican document credited Pius XII with working behind the scenes to save the lives of hundreds of thousands of Jews and argued that to have openly spoken out against the Shoah would have merely endangered the lives of millions of Catholics without helping any Jews. Cornwell found this argument not credible.

"That failure to utter a candid word about the Final Solution in progress proclaimed to the world that the Vicar

of Christ was not moved to pity and anger. From this point of view, he was the ideal pope for Hitler's unspeakable plan. He was Hitler's pawn. He was Hitler's pope," he wrote.

Sister Margherita Marchione, an American nun and author who has written several books defending Pius, has rejected charges such as those leveled by Cornwell, Carroll, Gary Wills and other authors. "His actions—sheltering Jews in the Vatican and in the papal summer home in Castel Gandolfo; ordering that convents, monasteries, hospitals and schools shelter Jews; the issuing of false baptismal certificates, false identity papers and passports as well as providing money for ransom and travel to other countries—must not be underestimated," she said.

John Paul has himself defended Pius as "a great pope" and believes his predecessor has been maligned.

With Israeli Prime Minister Yitzhak Rabin, the year before he was assassinated, March 17, 1994. Vatican photo

In an effort to clear up the controversy, the Vatican in 1999 convened a commission of three Jewish and three Catholic historians to look at the record. But the effort backfired, producing more bitterness. In July 2001 the commission suspended its activities following the Vatican's refusal to open its wartime archives for its examination. The commission had prepared a preliminary report raising searing questions the scholars said could not be answered without access to more archival material. The Vatican said it had nothing to hide, but the archives could not be opened, probably for several years, until it had completed cataloging all the documents.

Despite these painful disagreements, many involved on either side of the Catholic–Jewish dialogue were confident their relationship was sturdy enough to resist such strains. They expressed faith that the changes Pope John Paul and his Jewish interlocutors had wrought were largely irreversible and would stand as an enduring monument to his pontificate. But others remained wary, warning that it was naïve and unrealistic to believe that the tormented history of 2,000 years could be completely negated within a single generation. If the next pope were to declare a renewal in efforts to convert Jews, much of the work of the past 20 years would be undone.

For Jews, the central question to be put to Christians remained, in the words of Rabbi Michael Signer, "Can we trust you, can we trust you now?" For Pope John Paul, the answer was a resounding yes. It will be for his successor to provide an answer for the future.

In memory of Adolph and Bertha Elsner, killed at Belzec extermination camp, Poland, August 1942.

In His Own Words

"I'm all in one piece. I'm not dead yet," during his first public audience after falling and dislocating his shoulder in 1993.

"I have understood what exploitation is, and I have immediately put myself on the side of the poor, the disinherited, the oppressed, the marginalized and defenseless. The powerful in this world do not always look favorably on a pope like that," interview with Polish-Italian journalist Jas Gawronski in 1993.

"You have to admire my loyalty," quipping to medical staff at Rome's Gemelli hospital, where he was admitted in 1994 for the sixth time in his pontificate to repair a broken thigh bone.

"I declare that the Church has no authority whatsoever to confer priestly ordination on women and that this judgment is to be definitively held by all the Church's faithful," from a 1994 letter in which he confirmed the ban on women priests.

"To this day, Auschwitz does not cease to admonish, reminding us that anti-Semitism is a great sin against humanity, that all racial hatred inevitably leads to the trampling of human dignity," speaking of the Nazi death camp in his 1994 book *Crossing the Threshold of Hope.*

"They say the pope is getting old and that he can't walk without a cane, but in one way or another, I'm still around. My hair is still intact, and things are not so bad with my head either. You must say about me—not only was he the pope, but he skied and canoed—and who knows what else! And he even broke his leg sometimes," to Polish bishops in January 1995.

Pope John Paul prays at the Holocaust memorial
Umschlagplatz in Warsaw. The memorial marks the place
where Jews were rounded up and escorted to the
concentration camps of World War Two, June 11, 1999.
Vincenzo Pinto/Reuters

The land of milk and honey. Looking out from Jordan's
Mount Nebo, from where Moses first saw the promised land,
March 20, 2000. Vatican photo

With Israeli rabbis Meir Lau and Eliahu Bakshi-Doran in
Jerusalem, March 23, 2000. Radu Sigheti/Reuters

Honoring the dead. At the Yad Vashem memorial to Holocaust
victims, Jerusalem, March 23, 2000. Jim Hollander/Reuters

Yad Vashem, Jerusalem, March 23, 2000. Jim Hollander/Reuters

At the Western Wall, March 26, 2000. Jim Hollander/Reuters

A difficult dialogue. The pope sits between Israel's Chief Rabbi Meir Lau and Muslim cleric Sheikh Tayseer Al-Tamimi in Jerusalem. The Jewish leader and the Muslim cleric did not shake hands and Tayseer left early without taking part in a tree-planting ceremony, March 23, 2000. Radu Sigheti/Reuters

With Rabbi Yaakov Dov Bleich at the Babi Yar Jewish
monument in Kiev, Ukraine, June 25, 2001. Vincenzo
Pinto/Reuters

A Paradoxical Papacy

Tom Heneghan

It was a summit that no emperor, king or president could call. On October 27, 1986, Pope John Paul II invited leaders of the world's religions to assemble in Assisi, birthplace of the gentle Saint Francis, to pray for peace. Dozens of Jewish, Muslim, Protestant, Orthodox, Buddhist and Sikh clerics made the pilgrimage to the central Italian town. African animists and Japanese Shintoists also heeded the call. The prayer meeting celebrated the unity of believers and the diversity of their beliefs, displayed by guests ranging from the Dalai Lama of Tibet and Anglican Archbishop of Canterbury Robert Runcie to John Pretty-on-Top, a Crow Indian medicine man from Montana. It was a moving testimony to faith despite differences, and the head of the world's largest single church stressed the good they could do together. "Either we learn to walk together in peace and harmony or we drift apart and ruin ourselves and others," John Paul told his guests.

That same year, the Vatican took a different approach to differences within the Catholic Church itself. It stripped Father Charles Curran of his tenured post as professor of moral theology at Catholic University in Washington, DC, because he challenged Church teachings on sexual morality. It ordered a California Jesuit to put aside a survey he was taking of American bishops' views on priestly celibacy and women's ordination, two other issues where the pope brooked no debate. The Jesuit later left the priesthood. The U.S. church was not the only one in the Vatican's sights. Early in John Paul's papacy, Rome disciplined Latin America's "liberation theology" school and appointed conservative bishops to confront it. Sanctions against other theologians, especially Europeans and Asians, were yet to come.

John Paul's pontificate has been a study in contrasts. Never before has the Church had such a high-profile pope bringing Christ's message to all parts of the globe. His tireless evangelizing has made him one of the world's best-known figures, an international leader defending a moral vision amid the world's strains and strife. Millions of people have flocked to hear him preach around the globe. Even the heads of officially atheistic regimes, such as former Soviet President Mikhail Gorbachev and Cuban leader Fidel Castro, have treated him with deep respect. His determination to continue preaching God's word despite advancing age and infirmity has deeply impressed Catholics and non-Catholics alike.

Within his Church of a billion souls, however, opinions have been as divided over John Paul's policies as they have been united about his personality. The Church represents for Catholics around the world a source of eternal values and moral authority. But their interpretation takes on many forms. Throughout his papacy, John Paul has fostered a strict orthodoxy that Vatican officials defend relentlessly. He has centralized decision-making in the Vatican to ensure local churches follow the Roman line. His critics chafe under the discipline, calling his style authoritarian. Liberal Catholics in Western countries dislike the traditional views he brought to the Vatican from his native Poland. But the pope's enthusiastic supporters say John Paul is doing exactly what a pontiff should do—guiding the Church with authority. They believe the Church should not change just to suit the times. Catholicism represents many truths about God, humans and the relationship between them, they say, and what has served it well for 2,000 years must continue in the future. George Weigel, a conservative American theologian and biographer of John Paul, speaks for these believers when he calls liberals part of a "wrecking crew" that, if left unchecked, would lead to a moral and doctrinal deconstruction of Catholicism.

This vigorous Catholicism that John Paul has defended against what he sees as the fads and false gods of the modern world has sometimes been jarring to non-Catholics who do not share the Vatican way of "thinking in centuries." The same religious leaders touched by his Assisi summit were hurt 14 years later when the Vatican, alarmed by what it considered some overly ecumenical theologians, said other faiths were "gravely deficient" and should not be called "sister churches" because Catholicism is the Mother Church of Christianity.

As these debates have raged, the Church and the world have changed in ways that John Paul could hardly have imagined when he was ordained a priest in 1946. Catholicism's center of gravity has shifted from Europe and North America to the Third World, especially Latin America, where religious fervor lives on. In Africa and parts of Asia, Christianity competes—sometimes violently—with Islam in a race to win souls from fading local religions. The Church faces a dramatic shortage of priests worldwide. In Western countries, where all forms of authority have come under scrutiny, confidence in the hierarchy has plummeted and critics call for a wide range of reforms. At the same time, despite the din of controversy and change, a vast flock of believers around the globe believes in and remains loyal to the world's largest church.

Quo vadis Ecclesia Christi?—where are you going, Church of Christ?—a Catholic might ask in the Church's official language, Latin. Here again, the answers differ. Some look at the human side and say it depends on who succeeds John Paul. Others stress the Church doctrine that the Holy Spirit guides the choice and policies of any pope. All agree, though, that any significant change will be slow in coming and that any other prediction about the next pontificate is a gamble. After the staunchly conservative Pius XII, for example, nobody could have guessed that the grandfatherly John XXIII would usher in sweeping reforms. The Second Vatican Council he opened in 1962 was a turning point that brought the Church into the modern age by opening up theological debate, replacing Latin with local languages at mass and inviting laypeople to play a larger role in their parishes. John Paul has packed the College of Cardinals with solidly conservative men expected to exercise caution, but that does not mean they will elect a new pontiff in his image. Whoever the next pope is, he will inherit a church deeply marked by John Paul's long reign and will have to find his own answers to the challenges facing it.

Open and Closed

One of John Paul's most outstanding qualities has been his rock-solid conviction in preaching a message that often went firmly against the spirit of the times. Previous chapters have recounted his role in defying communism in Poland and defending human rights around the world. When global stock markets were booming, the pope tirelessly criticized consumer society as shallow and ultimately unfulfilling. For the Jubilee Year 2000, he championed debt relief for Third World countries forgotten amid the market mania in the West. John Paul also advanced the dialogue between religions after Assisi by apologizing to Jews, Protestants, Orthodox and Muslims for wrongs done in the Church's name over the centuries. Whatever the issue, the pope has found a way to bring a deeper moral perspective to bear on it. As Father Thomas Reese, the liberal editor-in-chief of the Jesuit weekly *America*, put it, "John Paul II will go down in history as the most important world figure in the second half of the 20th century. He was simply the right man at the right place at the right time."

John Paul's calls for freedom around the world have not always echoed within his Church. Judging that liberals had pushed the Vatican II reforms too far, he has re-exerted papal control over Catholic universities and reduced the power of local churches to decide some policy matters on their own. The Congregation for the Doctrine of the Faith, the Vatican's theological watchdog department, has disciplined prominent theologians for challenging Church teaching. Among them was Swiss theologian Hans Küng, who lost his right to teach Catholic theology at Germany's Tübingen University for questioning papal infallibility, just as Curran did for challenging teaching on sexual morality. Belgian Jesuit Jacques Dupuis was forced under Vatican pressure to disown some views on interreligious dialogue. Those who have been disciplined have accused the Congregation's head, German Cardinal Joseph Ratzinger, of being heavy handed.

"There is a fear of debate in the Church, and the suspicion that if we really air our disagreements, then the authority of the Church will be undermined," said Father Timothy Radcliffe, a Briton and former head of the Dominican order worldwide. "But I believe that nothing undermines the authority of the Church so much as the suspicion that we do not say what we believe…we cannot seek the truth unless we dare to play with ideas, try out crazy hypotheses to see where they take us, float a thought and chance our arm."

Dissent is only one part of a larger whole. Many other talented theologians agree with the steadfast course the pope has charted, but their names are not household words like those who have been disciplined. They do not see theological debate as a question of intellectual freedom neutral to Catholic tradition but as a disciplined intellectual effort to understand divine revelation. "All [theological] speculation must take place within a determined conviction to 'think with the Church' and with a clear understanding that the rule of faith is determined by the Church's pastors, not by the Church's theologians," Weigel has written. "Popes and bishops do not make things up as they go along. Doctrine is not a matter of papal or episcopal whim or willfulness. Popes and bishops are the servants, not the masters, of tradition—the truths—that make the Church what it is. Thus the pope and the bishops are authoritative teachers, not authoritarian despots."

Sofia, Bulgaria, May 23, 2002. Oleg Popov/Reuters

From the start of his papacy, John Paul made it clear he wanted the Church to challenge the secular world rather than adapt to it. He urged priests to wear their Roman collars with pride rather than don anonymous casual clothes whenever they left their churches. He has vociferously upheld a strict sexual morality—no sex before marriage, no artificial birth control, no communion for divorced Catholics and no remarriage in church after a divorce. "The answer to the current crisis will not be found in Catholic Lite," Weigel wrote in his latest book, *The Courage to Be Catholic*. "It will only be found in a classic Catholicism—a Catholicism with the courage to be countercultural, a Catholicism that has reclaimed the wisdom of the past in order to face the corruptions of the

The pope is the spiritual leader of more than one billion Catholics worldwide. Roman Catholicism is the majority religion in more than 50 countries

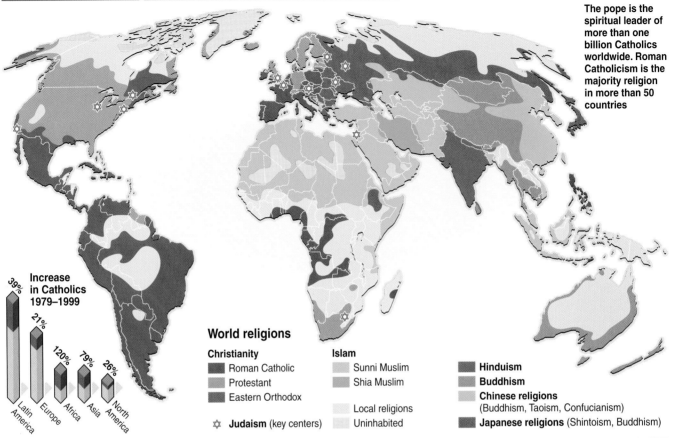

Increase in Catholics 1979–1999

39% Latin America
21% Europe
120% Africa
79% Asia
26% North America

World religions

Christianity
- Roman Catholic
- Protestant
- Eastern Orthodox

Islam
- Sunni Muslim
- Shia Muslim

- Local religions
- Uninhabited

☆ Judaism (key centers)

- Hinduism
- Buddhism
- Chinese religions (Buddhism, Taoism, Confucianism)
- Japanese religions (Shintoism, Buddhism)

Worldwide adherents of selected major religions, 2000

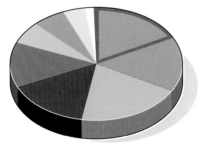

Millions	Africa	Asia	Europe	Latin America	North America	World
▢ Roman Catholics	120.39	118.71	285.98	461.22	71.04	1,057.34
▨ All Christians	360.23	337.96	559.64	481.10	260.62	1,999.55
▨ Muslims	317.37	833.18	31.57	1.67	4.45	1,188.24
▨ Atheists and nonreligious	5.44	734.20	130.76	18.69	30.15	919.24
▨ Hindus	2.35	805.48	1.42	0.77	1.33	811.35
▨ Chinese religionists	0.03	383.47	0.26	0.19	0.85	384.80
▨ Buddhists	0.13	354.95	1.55	0.65	2.70	359.98
▨ Local religionists	96.81	128.57	1.26	1.29	0.44	228.37
▢ New religionists*	0.09	100.64	0.16	0.62	0.84	102.35
▨ Jews	0.21	4.53	2.53	1.14	6.02	14.43

Sources: Encyclopedia Britannica World Book; Catholic Missionary Union of England and Wales; World Almanac 2002

* Followers of Asian 20th Century New Religions, New Religious movements, radical new crisis religions, and non-Christian syncretistic mass religions, all founded since 1800 and mostly since 1945

present and create a renewed future, a Catholicism that risks the high adventure of fidelity."

The challenge is stirring. It rings true to many older Catholics brought up in the discipline of the pre-1960s Church as well as a growing number of younger Catholics around the world who see a return to traditional values as the answer to their own searing questions about their faith. It clearly stands as a challenge before the millions of youths who turn out for the World Youth Days, the global "Catholic Woodstock" held every two years. They cheer on the aging pope like a rock star and pack the vast open air masses he celebrates. But do they obey all that he says? A poll before the 1997 World Youth Day in Paris showed three-quarters of French youths surveyed disagreed with his stand on AIDS, contraception and abortion. About 80 percent of American and 90 percent of German Catholics think birth control is a matter of each individual's conscience, polls show. "He simply has not won people over on birth control," Reese observed. "He continues to teach but the students aren't listening."

The Church has suffered a steep decline in both mass attendance and vocations in Western countries since the 1960s. In once solidly Catholic Ireland, mass attendance has fallen from 90 percent back then to about 50 percent overall now, with much lower rates in cities like Dublin. The same trend has pushed churchgoing in the United States down from half to a quarter since 1972. It is down as low as 10 percent in European countries like France. In a telling trend, the Polish church, which fought off oppressive communism so successfully, has seen its pews grow emptier on Sunday mornings since democracy and consumerism arrived.

As for vocations, the Church faces an enormous challenge just to replenish the ranks of the clergy. The number of men joining or staying in the priesthood went into sharp decline after Vatican II. This downward slide seems to have ended—the total number of priests went up in 1999 for the first time since 1978—but Catholic populations around the world have continued to grow steadily. With the average age of priests in the West over 60, the ranks of the clergy will again thin out dramatically over the next 10 to 20 years due to retirement and death. The Vatican yearbook *Annuario Pontificio 2002* shows there was a net increase of only 189 priests worldwide in 2001, leaving 405,178 priests

to serve more than a billion Catholics. Seminaries are closing in Ireland, a country that once dispatched priests around the world. In the United States, 27 percent of all parishes have no priest; in Europe, figures are over 30 percent. Because of the priest shortage, the traditional flows of missionaries around the world are shifting. Europeans once evangelized the colonies. Now, African and Asian priests move to Western Europe and North America to help run parishes there.

Belgian Cardinal Godfried Danneels has warned that Catholicism could eventually disappear from parts of Europe if it does not have enough priests to celebrate sacraments such as the Eucharist, baptism or marriage that are essential to Catholicism. "Without the sacraments, we'll become a Protestant church," he said. But those churches can hardly be a model, first of all for theological reasons but also because they too have suffered a steep erosion of their flocks. "The reform of the Catholic priesthood cannot mean making Catholic priests more like Anglican, Lutheran, Presbyterian, Methodist, Congregationalist or Unitarian clergy. It can only mean a reform in which Catholic priests become more intensely, intentionally and manifestly *Catholic*," Weigel argues.

The Universal Church

"Catholic" means universal. The diversity of the Church is on full display in St. Peter's Square every Easter Sunday during the pope's annual *Urbi et Orbi* ("to the city and to the world") address. A gifted linguist, John Paul reads out short messages in several dozen tongues to crowds waving flags from around the world. His pontificate has been a long and sustained effort to keep this worldwide church under firm central rule. Some bishops say their national conferences are not listened to in the curia, the Vatican bureaucracy, as they would like. "The curia treats us like altar boys," Chicago's late Cardinal Joseph Bernardin once complained.

A crucial factor in the unity-versus-diversity debate is the fact that the Church, which spent the first 1,500 years of its existence focused mostly on Europe, has shifted its center of gravity to the Third World. Now, 40 percent of all Catholics live in Latin America, 27 percent in Europe, 12 percent in Africa, 10 percent in Asia and nine percent in North America. This has led to a growing North-South split in outlook, with voices in some parts of Europe and North America calling for change slipping ever further into the minority as the more fervent traditional strains of Third World Catholicism gain the numerical upper hand. A quick tour around the world reveals a wide variety of local churches, each with its own challenges for the Vatican and for the man who will succeed John Paul.

North America

Scandal swept through the U.S. Church early in 2002 when it emerged that the Boston Archdiocese had been quietly reassigning child-molesting priests to new parishes for years without warning parishioners. The sordid stories of trusted men taking advantage of innocents shocked the faithful and led to calls for Cardinal Bernard Law to resign. Outrage followed when abuse cases emerged elsewhere in the country and the Church used cold legal defenses to protect errant priests and irresponsible bishops. The Vatican hardly helped either, initially hinting this was an "American problem" arising from a sex-soaked society, rapacious lawyers and leering anti-Catholic media.

Under pressure by abuse victims and unrelenting media coverage, the U.S. bishops struggled to respond to the

A Church in turmoil. Two girls protest against Boston's Cardinal Bernard Law, who was caught up in the U.S. Church's pedophilia scandal, April 28, 2002. Jim Bourg/Reuters

Cardinal Bernard Law of Boston, July 23, 2002.
Jim Bourg/Reuters

scandal. John Paul summoned American cardinals to the Vatican for emergency consultations in April 2002. At a crisis meeting in June, the bishops branded sexual abuse a "cancer" on the Church and agreed to bar errant clerics from any public ministry. Angry victims cried that this stopped short of the "zero tolerance" policy they demanded, which would exclude any cleric credibly accused of sex abuse from working as a priest. They were further disappointed when the Vatican rejected the U.S. guidelines, saying they were legally ambiguous and made accused priests guilty until proven innocent. They also left no room for Christian virtues like repentance and forgiveness, for example in the case of a one-time offender. The bishops went back to the drawing board, working out new guidelines with the Vatican that allowed for dismissals of errant clerics.

But the scandal refused to die down. In early December, Law flew off unannounced to Rome. On December 13, Law's black Friday, the pope accepted his resignation and named a special administrator to run the Boston Archdiocese temporarily. The scandal left deep distrust in its wake. Law admitted as much in his last statement as archbishop of Boston, saying he hoped his departure would lead to healing. "It is my fervent prayer that this action may help the Archdiocese of Boston to experience the healing, reconciliation and unity which are so desperately needed. To all those who have suffered from

Angry mothers. Protesters demonstrate on Mothers' Day in Boston against Cardinal Bernard Law over his handling of the American pedophilia scandal, May 12, 2002. Jim Bourg/Reuters

my shortcomings and mistakes I both apologize and from them beg forgiveness."

Many felt it was too little, too late.

Europe

The traditional heartland of the Church has become one of the most secular regions in the world. Mass attendance and vocations have dropped off dramatically. In many countries, people only turn to the Church for life's major rituals like baptism, marriage and funerals. The pope's policy of appointing deeply conservative bishops may have widened the gulf between the hierarchy and the laity, especially in countries with strong Protestant influence, such as Germany, Switzerland and the Netherlands. By contrast, it has only enhanced the Church's position in traditionally Catholic countries, such as Italy, Spain and Portugal. Fast-growing "new ecclesial movements," which call on laypeople to live their faith in everyday life, also

Addressing U.S. Catholic leaders summoned to the Vatican to discuss the American pedophilia scandal, April 23, 2002. Vatican photo

have cheered John Paul. Best known among them are the conservative Opus Dei and the neo-catechumenates, both of which began in Spain, and Italian groups such as Communion and Liberation, Focolare and the Sant'Egidio Community.

Once a model of popular piety, Ireland has been rocked by a decade of sex abuse scandals that toppled priests from their pedestals and made them objects of public ridicule. It started with Bishop Eamonn Casey, who admitted in 1992 to an affair with a divorcee that produced an illegitimate son. Cases of priests abusing boys emerged throughout the 1990s in Ireland as well as other countries, such as Germany, France and Austria. The sex abuse issue rarely comes up in several other countries with long Catholic heritages, raising suspicion that old habits of secrecy and deference to the clergy still prevail there. Italy has no public guidelines for dealing with child abusers even though a handful of priests have been jailed for pedophilia. In the pope's native Poland, Poznan Archbishop Juliusz Paetz had to step down in early 2002 after being accused of sexually harassing seminarians and young priests.

Latin America

John Paul made his first papal voyage in 1979 to Mexico to read the riot act to the liberation theology movement then popular across Latin America. This grassroots brand of Catholicism stressed the revolutionary nature of Christ's message and advocated radical action to help the poor. Despite his public role in Poland, the pope told priests to stay out of politics. He also began appointing conservatives to the local hierarchy and gradually isolated liberation theology activists.

The Marxist rhetoric is gone, but social justice remains a top priority for the Church in Latin America. The poverty and misery of millions of Catholics living in economies buffeted by globalization are far too pressing an issue for the clergy to ignore. Even bishops who are conservative on many theological issues take a more liberal line in social policy, adding a distinctive Third World perspective to the worldwide Church.

Even so, the faithful in the once solidly Catholic region have been deserting the Church in alarming numbers for Protestant churches, especially those in the lively evangelical movement. Some converts found the spiritual experience more intense, others welcomed the evangelicals' puritan ethic. Women liked the way the Protestants rejected traditional Latin machismo in favor of more balanced relations between the sexes. Brazil, the world's largest Catholic country, is now about 20 percent Protestant, which makes it the world's third-largest Protestant country after the United States and Germany. Often helped by rich U.S. evangelical churches and governments keen to weaken the Catholics' social agenda, Protestants are making inroads in other Latin American countries as well.

Even though it suffers from a dramatic shortage of priests, Latin America accounts for 40 percent of world Catholicism and counts as the future center of the Church. With Latin American cardinals now outnumbering the Italians in the College of Cardinals, speculation about the next pope inevitably brings up the question of whether the next pontiff will have a Spanish or Portuguese surname.

Africa

Catholicism expanded steadily in black Africa during the 20th century, growing from two percent of the population in 1900 to 17 percent at the millennium. Seminaries in countries like Nigeria are full of candidates for the priesthood. The continent is also a prime region for conversions because local animist religions are slowly giving way to monotheistic Christianity and Islam. The rivalry between these two great religions can trigger bloody confrontations, such as the riots in Nigeria in November 2002 that killed at least 215 people after Muslims protested against holding the Miss World beauty contest in their country.

The local church has been implicated in Africa's bloody conflicts, including allegations that Catholic and Protestant clergy joined in and sometimes led Hutus in slaughtering hundreds of thousands of minority Tutsi tribesmen. Despite these and other problems, thousands of Catholic missionaries and lay workers continue to run hospitals, schools and clinics throughout Africa. A number of political leaders there have admitted that their countries' health systems would collapse if not for the tireless work of the Church and its staff in Africa.

Passing on the spirit. Ordaining a new priest in St. Peter's
Basilica, April 21, 2002. Paolo Cocco/Reuters

Asia

Catholics are a tiny minority in Asia, with less than three percent of the total population and about two-thirds of them in the region's only majority Catholic country, the Philippines. The rest live deep in the shadow of three other major religions—Buddhism, Islam and Hinduism—and walk a tightrope between appearing too foreign and going so native as to lose their Catholic identity. Conversions are few, and the active evangelizing that John Paul promotes shocks many consensus-oriented Asians.

India, which now has more Jesuits than the United States, has proven a fertile ground for new thinking about relations between Christianity and other world religions. One theologian, the Belgian Jesuit Jacques Dupuis, developed the view during his 36 years of missionary work that Catholicism should not seek conversions in Asia but join other churches in discovering how they all share in God's grace and love. When he published a book on this in 1997, the Vatican suspended him from teaching and accused him of arguing that one religion was just as good as another. After a two-year probe, Dupuis acknowledged that his book contained confusing statements. Former Vienna Cardinal Franz König, a respected ex-head of the Vatican office for nonbelievers, publicly defended Dupuis. "My heart bleeds when I see such obvious harm being done to the common good of God's Church," said the 97-year-old Church elder statesman.

The mark of cane. Joking with his walking stick, Vatican City, November 28, 2001. Paolo Cocco/Reuters

Challenges Ahead

After a pontificate as long as John Paul's, the prospect of a new pope invariably sparks off speculation about the future. Liberals draw up mental lists of what they hope to see implemented. Conservatives think of the unfinished business another orthodox pontiff could tackle. Thanks to the way John Paul broke the "non-Italians need not apply" mold, any Catholic who follows Church events wonders where the next pope will come from. The Catholic Church as an institution thinks in centuries, however, and knows it has to keep a balance between tradition and innovation.

Whoever succeeds John Paul will face unfinished business on several fronts.

Collegiality

Within such a vast Church, one recurring issue is collegiality, shorthand for decentralizing decision-making from the Vatican to bishops around the world. The bishop of Rome, traditionally the *primus inter pares* (first among equals), now reigns like a monarch over all other bishops. "Central church offices, out of a concern for unity of the faith, have leadership concepts from the 19th century," Küng has complained. Reformers hope even conservatives in the College of Cardinals will have chafed at being "treated like altar boys" and will now agree to push the pendulum back toward more decentralization. "You have to hope their pastoral experience shows them there has to be change," said Curran.

This might seem like a purely administrative issue, but it can have very practical effects. In the 1990s, for example, the curia effectively took back from the bishops' conferences the power that Vatican II granted them to make certain adaptations to the liturgy. This was reflected in a decade-long struggle between the curia and English-speaking bishops about using nonsexist "inclusive language" in prayers—for example, using "humanity" for "mankind" or "brothers and sisters" instead of "brethren." Rome finally rejected that, insisting translations stick closer to the original Latin—much to the chagrin of women put off by the Church's male bias.

Vatican centralism is also a problem for those theologians who see their job of interpreting the Scriptures as a kind of research and development for the Church. "Theologians

Smoke and fire. Blessing the altar with incense on New Year's Day in St. Peter's Basilica, January 1, 2002. Dylan Martinez/Reuters

A prayer for Christian unity. With Archbishop of Canterbury George Carey at the Vatican, December 3, 1996.
Paolo Cocco/Reuters

Celibacy

The child abuse scandal has inevitably drawn attention to celibacy, even though the Church says the two should not be linked. This tradition dates back to the earliest days of Christianity and was made legally binding for the Western Church in 1129. Skeptics inside and outside the Church assume the rule that priests cannot marry or engage in sex can lead to errant behavior. But celibacy's many defenders say this is a misreading of one of Catholicism's trademarks. Noting that Jesus himself never married, the Church values celibacy as a gift from God that frees priests to devote their lives fully to serve Him. It believes that personal sin, and not celibacy, drives errant priests to abuse others sexually. "To blame the crisis of sexual abuse on celibacy is about as plausible as blaming adultery on the marriage vow or blaming treason on the Pledge of Allegiance," Weigel writes.

There are married priests in the Catholic Church, mostly in the distinctive Eastern rites, which have long allowed married men to be ordained. The Church has also ordained a small number of former Anglicans and Episcopalians who left their churches to protest against the ordination of women there. But it is hard to imagine a decision to abolish celibacy or even make it optional in the foreseeable future. One area where movement might come would be in the ordination of so-called *viri probati*, which is Latin for men of proven character. These would be pious married men in middle age or later. A 1995 meeting of priests' councils from around Europe urged Rome to open up the priesthood to viri probati.

The celibacy and child abuse issues have been further complicated by the question of homosexual priests. Conceptual clarity is crucial here. Although priests who abuse boys are often called pedophiles, the label does not actually fit most of them because the majority have not preyed on prepubescent targets. Strictly speaking, their acts are homosexual and not child abuse. In fact, most genuine pedophiles are heterosexuals and the crime takes place mostly in families. What is at issue here is whether gay men can observe celibacy as faithfully as straight men.

John Paul has said the Church must ensure men with deviant desires are not accepted in holy orders. If this means barring gays, there could be problems. There are gays in the priesthood already. "The main argument in favor of the ordination of gay men is far more

have to learn how to use contemporary philosophy and language and methods to explain the Gospel in the 21st century. That's going to require experiment and risk," said Reese. But under John Paul, he added, "The Vatican looks at these people like a public health department looking at an infectious disease. It wants to stamp it out quickly before it spreads, isolate and quarantine it so it does not spread through the Church."

The pope and his supporters see that view as part of the problem and not part of the solution. They think some dissidents have become media darlings who have done more harm than good in the Church. As a solution, Weigel has called for a thorough reform of the theological education of candidates for the priesthood to counter what he calls "the silly season" that dominated Catholic education, particularly in the United States, in the last decades of the 20th century. "The result, unfortunately, is that too many seminarians are taught to deconstruct the Catholic tradition before they have even learned what the tradition is," he wrote.

convincing than the arguments against it—namely, the real-life example of thousands of healthy and hard-working gay priests and bishops," Reese argued. "These men lead lives centered on Christ and in service to the Church—celebrating the sacraments, running parishes, schools and dioceses and carrying out every type of Christian ministry."

To support the opposing view, Father Andrew Baker, a member of the Vatican's Congregation for Bishops, wrote in Reese's journal *America* that homosexual tendencies were "aberrations" and that same-sex attraction was "disordered." This, he wrote, should be enough to be included among the prudent doubts that Church law requires seminary directors to exercise when admitting candidates. Bishop Wilton Gregory, the president of the U.S. bishop's conference, has expressed concern that heterosexual men might be put off from entering the priesthood if there were too much of a "homosexual atmosphere" in seminaries.

Women and the Laity

After the sexual revolution, feminism and increasing equality at school and work, some Catholics in developed countries complain the Church has a stained-glass ceiling barring women from becoming priests. There is no groundswell of women clamoring for ordination, and many women around the world do not want it, either for themselves or for other women. But the male-only rule can rankle, especially in Western countries with active women's liberation movements. Opinion polls in northern European countries show a majority of laypeople, male and female, would have no problems with a woman priest. That view is far less prevalent in traditionally Catholic countries such as Italy and Spain and in Latin America.

John Paul is convinced he cannot change something that Christ himself laid down by choosing only men as the original Twelve Apostles. The Church teaches that this was a divine decision, not simply a reflection of the male domination of society at the time of Jesus. "I declare that the Church has no authority whatsoever to confer priestly ordination on women and that this judgment is to be definitely held by all the Church's faithful," he declared in 1994 in an attempt to officially close all debate. Despite that strong statement, the debate has not died down.

Hail to the chief. A Swiss Guard salutes the pope, May 22, 2001. Paolo Cocco/Reuters

Even Milan's former Cardinal Carlo Maria Martini, who for years was the liberals' dream candidate for pope, is cautious about ordaining women. "If the Catholic Church were to admit women priests, suddenly we could have divisions a hundred times worse than that of Lefebvre," he once said, referring to the French archbishop excommunicated in 1988 and whose traditionalist movement has about 150,000 followers. "The pope has to

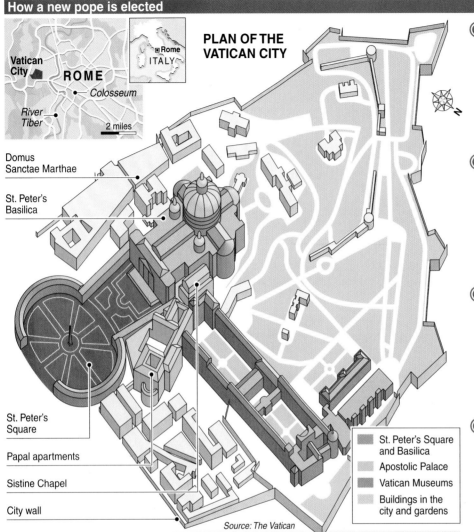

PLAN OF THE
VATICAN CITY

Vatican City

■Rome
ITALY

■Rome
ROME

Colosseum

River
Tiber

2 miles

Domus
Sanctae Marthae

St. Peter's
Basilica

St. Peter's
Square

Papal apartments

Sistine Chapel

City wall

Source: The Vatican

St. Peter's Square
and Basilica

Apostolic Palace

Vatican Museums

Buildings in the
city and gardens

① Death of the pope
The Camerlengo verifies and announces the pope's death. He seals the papal apartments and arranges for the papal ring and seal to be broken. He prepares for the pope's burial and the traditional nine days of mourning. Burial is between the fourth and sixth day after death. Popes are usually buried in St. Peter's Basilica

② Preparations for the election
Fifteen to 20 days after the death of the pope, the cardinals, who have traveled from all over the world, enter the Vatican "conclave" for the election. They are locked away from the outside world and must swear an oath of secrecy. They move from their accommodation in the Domus Sanctae Marthae to the Apostolic Palace for the voting process

③ The election process
The election is conducted by secret written ballot in the Sistine Chapel. The cardinals each receive a ballot paper, on which they write the name of their chosen candidate. After folding it, they approach the altar to place their ballot in a chalice. The votes are then counted and the ballots burned, producing the famous smoke. Chemicals are added to make it black or white

④ The result
The cardinals vote on the afternoon of the first day, then twice each morning and once each afternoon until a result is declared. To be elected pope, a candidate must receive more than two-thirds of the votes. If 30 elections have taken place without a result, the cardinals may elect by simple majority. The final ballots are burned and white smoke rising from the Vatican signals to a waiting world that a new pope is elected

⑤ The new pope
The Dean of the Cardinals asks if the successful candidate accepts election and by what name he wishes to be called as pope. When he agrees, a senior cardinal steps onto the main balcony of the Vatican and declares to the world, "Habemus Papam!" ("We have a pope!")

WHO'S WHO IN THE ELECTION

Camerlengo
The head of the College of Cardinals, responsible for governing the Church during the interregnum. Assisted by three cardinals, he directs the election of the new pope

College of Cardinals
Assumes responsibility for day-to-day running of the Church and elects the new pope. Every cardinal under 80 years of age may vote, up to a maximum of 120

Cardinal Assistants
Three cardinals are chosen by lot from the cardinal electors to assist in the voting process. Three new assistants are chosen by lot every three days

Who may be elected?
Although for centuries only cardinals have been elected pope, in theory, any adult male Roman Catholic is a potential candidate for the papacy

be concerned with keeping this huge flock with all its different opinions together."

Immobility on the role of women could run another risk, however. "The Church has to be extremely careful that women do not become anticlerical, because if they do, then we're in real trouble," Reese argued. As mothers and teachers, women play a key role in transmitting the faith to the next generation of Catholics—maybe more so than the priest who only gets in 10 minutes of sermon time on Sunday. That transmission belt has been breaking down in recent decades as some women have grown disenchanted with a Church that they found tone-deaf to their requests. Catholic youths can seem remarkably ignorant about their Church—priests ruefully joke that many think Vatican II is the pope's summer residence. Some women who turn away from a Church they find sexist also stop bringing up their children in the faith. Many others continue to transmit the faith despite their differences with the hierarchy. Attitudes at the grassroots level are important because Catholic families are the main gardens where Catholic vocations grow. These nurseries need to be well tended over the long term, regardless of the debates of the day, so the Church can look forward to future generations of priests.

Allowing women to be ordained deacons, or lay assistants to priests, could be a major step toward raising their status in the Church. Laywomen already do much of the behind-the-scenes work in many parishes, from teaching catechism to organizing fund-raising dinners, without having any ordained role in the Church. The Vatican has been studying the issue of women deacons for years, but no change seems to be in the offing.

The women's issue is linked to the question of what role the laity should play in the Church. After centuries of the Church being seen as the hierarchy and clergy, Vatican II redefined it as "the people of God" and urged the faithful to play an active role in their parishes. This has had mixed success at the local level. At national consultations, the voice of the laity sometimes calls for reforms the Vatican says are not part of the Catholic tradition. The We Are Church movement, which began in Austria and Germany in the 1990s, now claims ties with 127 liberal Catholic groups in 27 countries. Conservative lay groups, such as the U.S.-based Catholic League, believe the liberals cause the problem. The Catholic League, for example, has a running battle with the liberal group Catholics for a Free Choice, calling it "an anti-Catholic organization" that does not deserve any legitimacy or media coverage.

Sexual Morality

The current gulf between the Church hierarchy and the laity opened in 1968 over issues of birth control. After the contraceptive pill further broke the link between sex and procreation, Vatican-appointed experts studied the birth control issue and found no doctrinal reason to condemn it. Pope Paul VI was undecided until the last minute and then ruled against their findings by issuing the encyclical *Humanae Vitae* banning contraception. Many laypeople around the world rejected the encyclical. Liberal priests openly criticized it. This was a major refusal of Catholics to go along with their hierarchy in modern times and opened a crack in the thick walls of obedience that had surrounded the Church until then.

In the years that followed, sexual morality turned into an issue on which many Catholics agreed to disagree with their Church. It is hard to say how many follow the Vatican on birth control, but the decline of the traditional large Catholic family in many Western countries is eloquent proof that many do not. Many priests avoid preaching about sexual morality from the pulpit, either because they know they have little credibility on this issue or they do not have the courage to tackle it. John Paul has vigorously preached the virtues of premarital chastity and natural family planning. Opinion polls show he has made little headway. One survey in 1998 found that support for the Church view that premarital sex is always wrong was down to 30 percent in Ireland and just under 20 percent in the United States, Poland and Italy.

While this is a defeat for the hierarchy, it is not really a victory for the laity. New sexual freedoms have brought new problems and the need for the guidance that people look to churches to provide. For example, modern science has not only developed birth control; it has also found new ways to help create life, such as artificial insemination and *in vitro* fertilization that offer hope for childless couples yearning to found a family. But the Vatican has opposed many of these options, and some believers find themselves in a dilemma. Catholics instinctively identify with their Church's traditional respect for life, love and family. Many also tend toward caution when faced with the confusing new options science presents. But some think that "just say no" is no longer enough of an answer to their questions.

Another issue where pressure is mounting for change is divorce. Catholics who divorce cannot receive communion at mass and are not allowed to remarry in church. With divorce among Catholic couples now ever more frequent in Western countries, churchgoers who've split up can feel branded and unwanted. Three German bishops, including national conference leader Cardinal Karl Lehmann, drew up guidelines in 1993 for changing the rules, but the Vatican rejected them.

Religious Tolerance

As the Assisi summit showed, the Church has probably never had a pontiff as open to cooperating with other religions as John Paul. His 1995 encyclical *Ut Unim Sint* (That They May Be One) boldly invited all Christian churches to discuss how the papacy that has divided them for so long could be used to bring them together. The pope has succeeded in patching up some doctrinal differences with the Lutherans dating back to the Reformation itself, and was making progress with the Anglicans until they decided to ordain women priests a decade ago. He told the Jews he believed their covenant with God remained valid, a major shift from the Church's traditional view that they had to be converted to be saved. John Paul began reaching out to Muslims early in his papacy. "Christians and Muslims—generally we have understood each other badly. Sometimes in the past we have opposed each other and even exhausted ourselves in polemics and wars. I believe that God is calling us today to change our old habits," he said during a visit to Casablanca, Morocco, in 1985. Sixteen years later in Damascus, he became the first pope to visit a mosque.

All these acts were welcomed as long overdue signs of respect for other peoples' deepest beliefs. But some statements from the Vatican's doctrinal office in recent years have included what critics call a "Catholic superiority complex," which they say contradicts some of John Paul's actions. In 1998, while arguing that non-infallible papal teaching was also binding on Catholics, the Vatican's Cardinal Ratzinger illustrated his point by noting the Church taught that ordinations in the Anglican Communion were invalid. Anglican clergy were hurt by the remark. The strongest blow came in September 2000, when Ratzinger issued a document entitled *Dominus Iesus* (Lord Jesus) that said other religions and denominations were "gravely deficient." Although aimed at countering an apparent trend toward religious relativism in Asia, this sternly worded document offended non-Catholics who felt it relegated them to the ranks of second-class Christians.

This blunt language can confuse Catholics as well. All over the world, Catholics live in societies where respect for other peoples and religions has become a daily way of life, even a civic duty. For example, migration has brought Muslims to Western Europe and North America in such large numbers that Islam is now the second-largest religion in such traditionally Catholic countries as France and Italy. Christ's example of tolerance is a powerful inspiration for Christians to be open to their new neighbors. But many saw *Dominus Iesus* as going against the spirit of the times.

Vatican III?

With so many outstanding problems, Church liberals are tempted to plumb for a new council—a Vatican III—to pick up the pace of reform again. Milan's Cardinal Martini cautiously floated the idea in 1999, and Cardinal Lehmann in Germany seconded it a year later. The French Catholic magazine *La Vie* published a poll in 2000 saying nine out of 10 practicing Catholics there wanted a new council to be called. Its main topics, they said, should be celibacy (58 percent), the place of laity and women in decision-making (45 percent), a resumption of ecumenism (43 percent), interreligious dialogue (41 percent) and the status of divorced people in the church (27 percent).

But what would a Vatican III achieve? There is no guarantee that another council would be as reform-minded as the last one was. Church conservatives, who were surprised by the audacity of Vatican II, would not go into another major review of Church policy without a clear agenda of how to promote their own views. As Cardinal Walter Kasper, a German prelate who thinks a new council is worth considering, remarked, "One argument against a new council is that we haven't even digested the last one."

The View from the Pew

The challenges confronting the Catholic Church will not be easy to face. John Paul's successor will have to address these and other issues to ensure the Church adapts to its third Millennium. Whatever he does, though, the new pope likely will do it at a measured pace, as befits the world's oldest continually running institution. In its 2,000 years, Catholicism has survived persecution under the Romans, the 11th century Great Schism that split Christianity into the eastern Orthodox and western Roman rites and the 16th century Reformation that further divided western Christianity into Catholics and Protestants. Once sovereigns over large parts of Italy and influential in the ruling houses of Europe, the popes now reign only over the tiny Vatican city state. Pontiffs have ranged from saints to sinners, from simple pious men to towering intellects, from introverted "prisoners of the Vatican" to the charismatic globetrotter that John Paul has been. But the institution, with all its human failings, endures.

It endures because Catholics look to the inspiration beyond the institution. Amid all the pressing crises and heated debate, huge numbers of Catholics around the world still attend mass, respect their priests and follow Church teachings as best they can. Catholic religious and laypeople run vast networks of schools, hospitals, social services and publications designed to serve others in this world. All this happens because, for the faithful in the pews on Sunday, the Church is above all a community where they can live their faith, voice their concerns and share their joys. It is where they hear the message of Jesus Christ, that God is love and love of God and neighbor is the path to salvation. And here, no matter what they may think about the debates that rage in the Church, is where they fully agree with Pope John Paul.

In His Own Words

"A nation that kills its own children has no future," issuing a cry to his countrymen in 1996, when Poland's parliament was dominated by ex-communists who wanted to make abortion available freely again. The move to liberalize abortion failed when the constitutional court ruled it illegal.

"Ever since I was a boy I was a great hiker. Then I became a great traveler, and I hope to continue to be one," responding to a boy who asked him at a Rome parish in 1996 why he could not stand still.

"Sometimes I would ask myself: 'So many young people of my own age are losing their lives. Why not me?' Today I know that it was not mere chance," writing in 1996 about his days as a young man in Nazi-occupied Poland during World War Two.

"People need to know that there is no place in the priesthood and religious life for those who would harm the young," addressing U.S. cardinals at a crisis meeting in April 2002 on child sex scandals involving U.S. priests.

"Violence never again! War never again! Terrorism never again! In the name of God, may every religion bring upon the earth justice and peace, forgiveness and life. Love," addressing a special peace meeting in Assisi, Italy, in 2002, after the September 11, 2001, attacks against the United States.

The Hill of Crosses, September 7, 1993

By Thomas Szlukovenyi

I reached Lithuania's Hill of Crosses near the city of Siauliai two hours before the pope was due to arrive there. At first I just stood there, overwhelmed by the sight—huge crosses and small ones, some carved from wood and others sculpted in metal. I was surrounded by every cross imaginable.

Legend has it that the placing of crosses there dated from the 13th century. The Hill of Crosses became a potent symbol of Lithuanian defiance in the face of oppression and foreign invaders. Before Lithuania became independent, Soviet security forces repeatedly tore down the crosses. But new forests of crosses reappeared.

There was particular poignancy in a pilgrimage to this special place by a pope from Poland who himself had struggled against oppression in his own land, just across the border.

I was determined to capture this extraordinary image by securing the best possible position, trying to guess the route the pope would take on his way to the top of the hill. I decided the best picture would be at the bottom of the hill where I could show a mass of crosses with the pope and his entourage walking among them. I squeezed in between a garbage can and an uncooperative policeman and spent the next two hours worrying if I had made the right choice. Most other photographers opted for different angles.

The moment the pope arrived and started his walk toward the historic hill, the sun came out, throwing the whole scene into backlight. Keeping one eye on the approaching pope I frantically adjusted the camera to the new conditions and was just in time to shoot two frames exactly as planned. What photographers call "contrasty" light gave the scene even more drama. I took the shots and hoped for the best.

To my immense relief, the film was fine when I got back to Vilnius, and the picture was sent to London for distribution around the world. I went to my bed that night knowing I had shot a picture I would long remember. I hoped others who saw it would remember it too.

Pope John Paul walks by the Hill of Crosses on his way to celebrate an outdoor mass in Siauliai, Lithuania. Lithuanians erected thousands of crosses in defiance of the Soviet communist regime, September 7, 1993. Tom Szlukovenyi/Reuters

The Vatican, August 8, 2001. Vincenzo Pinto/Reuters

Judgment day. Sitting under Michelangelo's Last Judgment fresco at the opening of the restored Sistine Chapel, December 11, 1999.
Paolo Cocco/Reuters

Christ and his vicar. Rome, August
20, 2000. Vincenzo Pinto/Reuters

Concentric views. Bishops surround the pope at the start of a synod, St. Peter's Basilica, 1994. Luciano Mellace/Reuters

A special welcome to the world. Baptizing Faustine Frichot of France in the Sistine Chapel, January 13, 2002. Dylan Martinez/Reuters

The weight of the Cross. At the Good Friday Way of the Cross procession at Rome's ancient Colosseum, April 13, 2001. Dylan Martinez/Reuters

A walk in the woods, Les Combes, Italy, July 16, 2000.
Claudio Papi/Reuters

The winds of Slovenia. Maribor, Slovenia, September 19, 1999.
Paolo Cocco/Reuters

Above the clouds. Assisi, Italy, January 3, 1998.
Paolo Cocco/Reuters

Associate Editor

Philip Pullella

Philip Pullella has been a correspondent for Reuters in Rome since 1983. He came to Italy in 1979 on the Agnelli Foundation fellowship for Italian–American journalists. He has accompanied Pope John Paul on more than 70 of his overseas trips as well as many trips in Italy. In the past two decades with Reuters in Rome, he also has covered the Italian political situation, natural disasters and Italian culture. A son of Italian immigrants, he grew up in Manhattan and was educated at Boston University, where he received a degree in journalism.

Writers

Alan Elsner

Born in London, Elsner emigrated to Israel in 1977. The first permanent Reuters correspondent in Jerusalem 1983–85, he was Chief Correspondent Nordic Countries (1987–89), State Department Correspondent (1989–94), Chief U.S. Political Correspondent (1994–2000) and U.S. National Correspondent (2000–present).

Tom Heneghan

In 25 years with Reuters, Heneghan has written about politics, economics, religion and war from over 30 countries. Major assignments included the fall of the Berlin Wall, Afghanistan's wars and the conflict in Kosovo. Born in 1951 in New York and educated by Jesuits there, he joined the agency as a trainee in 1977 and has worked in London, Vienna, Geneva, Islamabad, Bangkok, Hong Kong, Bonn and Paris. He is chief political correspondent for France based in Paris.

Sean Maguire

Sean Maguire has spent the last decade covering the collapse of Yugoslavia and the spread of democracy and market economics in eastern Europe. A Scot with a Jesuit education, Maguire has been based in Warsaw since 1998 as chief correspondent in Poland and then as Editor, Central and Eastern Europe. He reported on the pope's trips to Poland in 1999 and August 2002 and the first visit by the pontiff to Bulgaria, in May 2002.

Howard Goller

Deputy Editor of the Reuters World Desk in London, Goller reported on war and peace for 18 years from the Israeli–Palestinian front line where he was Reuters Deputy Bureau Chief and headed the Foreign Press Association. Educated at Northwestern University and Yale Law School, Goller also teaches journalism.

Paul Holmes

Holmes worked in Rome from 1987 to 1989. He returned as chief correspondent from 1994 to 1997 and during that time accompanied the pope on several foreign trips. He has reported from 40 countries and has covered major political developments in Europe and the Middle East. He is Reuters Editor, Political and General News, and lives in New York.

Frances Kerry

Kerry has been a correspondent in the Miami bureau since 2000. Before that, she worked for Reuters in Washington, Havana, Paris, Nairobi, Madrid, New Delhi and London.

Luciano Mellace

Luciano Mellace, 72, is one of Italy's most respected news photographers. He started working for Reuters in 1985. He covered five papacies and when he retired in 1996, the Vatican awarded him with the "Pro Ecclesia et Pontifice" medal, making him one of the few non-Vatican employees to receive it.

David Storey

Storey was Reuters correspondent in Warsaw in the early 1980s and covered two trips by Pope John Paul to his homeland. A specialist in foreign affairs and national security issues, he has worked in some 40 countries and is now based in Washington, DC.

Thomas Szlukovenyi

Thomas Szlukovenyi was born in Budapest, Hungary, in 1951. He joined Reuters in Vienna in 1990 as photographer Eastern Europe and became Chief Photographer of the former Soviet Union in 1993 based in Moscow. He moved to London as Editor in Charge and Senior Photographer for Europe in 1996, then became deputy Pictures Editor in Singapore. In August 2000, Szlukovenyi was appointed News Editor Asia, Pictures.

Graphics Journalist

Mike Tyler

A freelancer for Reuters News Graphics in London since 1997, Tyler studied graphic design at John Moores University, Liverpool, and worked on a range of corporate identity projects before establishing Mapstyle, a custom map design service, in 1994.

Researcher

David Cutler

David Cutler is senior Researcher at Reuters Editorial Reference Unit in London. Born in Glasgow, Cutler earned his degree in Information Science and started his career as an assistant at London's Imperial War Museum. In 1980 he joined the BBC as a researcher, offering backup to program makers; he started in Reuters in late 1987, becoming part of the Editorial Reference Unit team in 1990. The unit, which Cutler leads, provides research and information for journalists in London as well as bureaus around the world.

Photographers

Jim Bourg	Santiago Lyon
Will Burgess	Dylan Martinez
Andy Clark	Nancy McGirr
Paolo Cocco	Luciano Mellace
Bogdan Cristel	Claudio Papi
Jack Dabaghian	Alessia Pierdomenico
Alexander Demianchuk	Vincenzo Pinto
Zoraida Diaz	Oleg Popov
Dimitar Dilkoff	Max Rossi
Eric Gaillard	Oscar Sabetta
Paul Hanna	Mona Sharaf
Gary Hershorn	Radu Sigheti
Jim Hollander	Tom Szlukovenyi
Yiorgos Karahalis	Mario Tapia
Pawel Kopczynski	Arthur Tsang
Reinhard Krause	Leszek Wdowinski
Jerry Lampen	Rick Wilking
Mal Langsdon	Andrew Winning
Havakuk Levison	